PENGUIN CLASSICS

THE BHAGAVAD GITA

LAURIE L. PATTON is Charles Howard Candler Professor of Early Indian Religions at Emory University. Her scholarly interests are in the interpretation of early Indian ritual and narrative, comparative mythology, literary theory in the study of religion and women and Hinduism in contemporary India. In addition to over forty articles in these fields, she is the author or editor of seven books: *Authority, Anxiety, and Canon: Essays in Vedic Interpretation* (ed., 1994); *Myth as Argument: The Brhaddevata as Canonical Commentary* (author, 1996); *Myth and Method* (ed., with Wendy Doniger, 1996); *Jewels of Authority: Women and Text in the Hindu Tradition* (ed., 2002); *Bringing the Gods to Mind: Mantra and Ritual in Early Indian Sacrifice* (author, 2005) and *The Indo-Aryan Controversy: Evidence and Inference in Indian History* (ed., with Edwin Bryant, 2005). Her book of poetry, *Fire's Goal: Poems for a Hindu Year*, was published by White Clouds Press in 2003. She is completing research for another forthcoming book, *Grandmother Language: Women and Sanskrit in Maharashtra and Beyond*. At Emory, she has served as Winship Distinguished Research Professor in the Humanities (2003–6) and Chair of the Department (2000–2007).

The Bhagavad Gita

Translated by LAURIE L. PATTON

PENGUIN BOOKS

To my Hindu students, who kept us all thinking

PENGUIN CLASSICS

Published by the Penguin Group
Penguin Books Ltd, 80 Strand, London WC2R 0RL, England
Penguin Group (USA) Inc., 375 Hudson Street, New York, New York 10014, USA
Penguin Group (Canada), 90 Eglinton Avenue East, Suite 700, Toronto, Ontario, Canada M4P 2Y3
(a division of Pearson Penguin Canada Inc.)
Penguin Ireland, 25 St Stephen's Green, Dublin 2, Ireland (a division of Penguin Books Ltd)
Penguin Group (Australia), 250 Camberwell Road, Camberwell, Victoria 3124, Australia
(a division of Pearson Australia Group Pty Ltd)
Penguin Books India Pvt Ltd, 11 Community Centre, Panchsheel Park, New Delhi – 110 017, India
Penguin Group (NZ), 67 Apollo Drive, Rosedale, North Shore 0632, New Zealand
(a division of Pearson New Zealand Ltd)
Penguin Books (South Africa) (Pty) Ltd, 24 Sturdee Avenue, Rosebank, Johannesburg 2196, South Africa

Penguin Books Ltd, Registered Offices: 80 Strand, London WC2R 0RL, England

www.penguin.com

First published in Penguin Classics 2008

001

Set in 10.25/12.25 pt PostScript Adobe Sabon
Typeset by Rowland Phototypesetting Ltd, Bury St Edmunds, Suffolk
Printed in the United States of America

ISBN: 978-0-140-44790-3

Contents

Acknowledgements

Several sojourners have helped me along this path: my students Michelle Roberts, Suhas Sridharan, Luke Whitmore, Peter Valdina, Lisa Crothers, Antoinette Denapoli, Arthi Devarajan, Harshita Mruthinti, Diana Rowe and Alicia Sanchez. My colleagues (mentors and peers alike) have commented on drafts and discussed larger issues of translation: Gayatri Chatterjee, Narendra Panjwani, G.U. Thite, Gyan Pandey, Ruby Lal, Sara McLinctock, Arindam Chakravarti, Jack Hawley, Arshia Sattar, Paul Courtright, Gary Tubb, Vasu Narayanan, Kathryn McClymond, Linda Hess, V. Narayana Rao, Timothy Lubin, Wendy Doniger, David Shulman, Graham Schweig, Purushottama Bilimoria, David Eckel, Brad Herling, Madhavi Kolhatkar, Pushpa Kale, Asha Gurjar and Maitreyee Deshpande. Deans Robert Paul and Cris Levenduski provided much needed sabbatical time.

Joyce Flueckiger, Nadine Berardi, and Shalom Goldman deserve special thanks, as does John Hinnells, the commissioning editor of the series. A grant from the American Council of Learned Societies (in collaboration with the National Endowment for the Humanities and Social Science Research Council) in 2004 allowed me to discuss this translation with several participants in my research project on women and Sanskrit. The final phase of this translation was completed with the support of the Fox Center for Humanistic Inquiry at Emory University, and the Sweetwater Group, Sautee, Georgia.

Introduction

BEGINNING TO READ

The *Gita* is about a decision.[1] Above all, it is about a decision to go to war. Arjuna wonders, as perhaps all warriors do, about the identity of his enemies, and his ties to them. 'With whom must I fight?' he asks Krishna, a prince from a neighbouring kingdom, who acts as his confidant and charioteer. Arjuna must grasp the heartbreaking fact that his enemies are his uncles, teachers and cousins. And when Arjuna grasps this fact, the decision he faces renders him speechless and broken.

Krishna's response to Arjuna takes the shape of what Indian Sanskrit tradition calls a *samvada* – a dialogue or conversation, in which options for action are explored, the meanings of those potential actions weighed carefully and teachings given. The *Gita* is a conversation in which Arjuna's very being is transformed by his encounter with Krishna. Initially, Arjuna's attention is captured by the sagacity of the advice that Krishna is giving. Over time, however, Arjuna understands that Krishna is, in fact, not simply a friend who helps him in a crisis, but a manifestation of God himself. The conversation between Arjuna and Krishna not only changes the course of the battle in which they are engaged, but changes the stories they tell about themselves and their world.

Most great literature, whether oral or written, revolves around the intricacies of a decision. Hamlet's 'To be or not to be' soliloquy is well known in Western European and American cultures. In the ancient Mesopotamian *Epic of Gilgamesh*, Gilgamesh must decide whether to seek immortality. In the early modern European text of *Don Quixote*, the hero Quixote must make a decision about leaving his estate and venturing out into the world. And such decisions require a whole array of resources – philosophy, poetry, history, ethics and even song. In great literature, a decision can be a prism through which a culture is refracted into different modes of expression. So, too, with the *Gita*: its contents include simple and moving poetry, dense philosophy, moral musing and an explosive description of God.

The *Gita*'s greatness lies in these multiple modes of expression. As Tzvetan Todorov reminds us, a symbol is a sign that constantly invites interpretation, and the symbols of the *Gita* have yet to exhaust the energies of whose who wish to interpret it. In the last century, when both Western and Indian readers have had access to it, it has become a world classic, spawning a myriad of translations, commentaries, renderings, paraphrases and synopses. Through the centuries, the *Gita* has remained a relevant text, inspiring militant revolutionaries, non-violent truth-seekers and renouncers of the world. It has enlightened German philosophers such as Schopenhauer and Heidegger; it has inspired Victorian poets such as Sir Edwin Arnold; and it has grounded post-Independence philosophers such as Sarvapelli Radhakrishnan. It has become a literary 'site' which decision-makers turn to to understand their dilemmas, whether they be Indian women and men leading Gandhi's *satyagraha*, twenty-first-century South Asian-American officers deciding to go to war in the Gulf, or London housewives with their children deciding how to organize their day.

The *Gita* also beckons for each generation to interpret it afresh; its language and imagery are flexible enough to be inspiring to those who must make new kinds of decisions. These readers confront new kinds of public and private despair, despair similar enough to Arjuna's for his world-shattering conversation with Krishna to still seem compelling. While the *Gita* gives us some of the basic contours of our human dilemmas, each generation must weave again the complex fabric that the *Gita* began to weave more than two millennia ago – a fabric of duty and love, action and inaction, divine and human.[2]

WHO: THE CHARACTERS AND PERSONALITIES OF THE *MAHABHARATA*

The participants in this dialogue are central characters in the great Hindu epic, the *Mahabharata*, which took recognizable form in the two centuries before and the two centuries after the Common Era. Arjuna, the despondent one, is a warrior and a member of the *kshatriya varna*, the class of people whose duty it is to protect the kingdom and its citizens. Arjuna belongs to the Pandava side of the Bharata family, the descendants of Pandu, the 'Pale One', who was cursed to die if he had intercourse with a woman.

Pandu's wife is the strong and wise Kunti, who, because of Pandu's curse, asked three different gods to impregnate her instead (Pandu's second wife, Madri, did the same). Arjuna's father is the warrior god Indra, a tempestuous deity known in the Vedas, the earliest Indian compositions. Arjuna inherits his father's valour in battle, and possesses a deep sense of righteousness and justice. Arjuna has also been trained by the Hindu god Shiva in the use of magical weapons, and possesses knowledge of the right mantra to deploy them. Arjuna knows when to fight and when to refrain from fighting; indeed, restraint, self-control and non-violence were essential to the warrior code.

Arjuna is one of five brothers, all of whom play a role in the impending great war. Yudhishthira, the eldest, is the son of Dharma, or Sacred Duty personified. Yudhishthira's strength is his capacity for discernment between right and wrong. Bhima, Arjuna's younger brother, is the strong son of the wind god Vayu, and quick to anger when he perceives injustice in a fight. Nakula and Sahadeva, the youngest, are twin sons of Madri (Pandu's second wife), and skilled in the arts of healing. The Pandavas also have an unknown half-brother, Karna, Kunti's son by the sun god, Surya. Karna was born before Kunti was married, and was abandoned by her and brought up by a charioteer. Karna sides with the Kauravas, the Pandavas' enemies, during the war. The Pandavas also share a wife, Draupadi, daughter of King Drupada, an ally from a great neighbouring kingdom. All the family members' wisdom must come to bear on Arjuna as he makes this decision: discernment, prowess and healing all play a crucial role in his dialogue with Krishna.

Throughout their childhood together, the Pandavas endure a tense relationship with their cousins, the Kauravas. They grow up in the same royal household of their kingdom, Hastinapura. The Kauravas are also of the Bharata lineage, but their father is a blind king, Dhritarashtra. The eldest, Duryodhana, has felt competitive with and slighted by his Pandava cousins since they grew up in the same palace, practising martial arts with the same teacher, Drona, and learning sacred lore from the same wise great-uncle, Bhishma. Both Pandavas and Kauravas stand to inherit the kingdom of Hastinapura. As adults, many kinds of encounters between the two sets of cousins increase the Kauravas' jealousy. After several attempts to ruin his cousins, Duryodhana's envy grows so great that he challenges the Pandavas to a dice game, knowing that Yudhishthira's one weakness is his love of gambling.

Yudhishthira is filled with illusions about his capacity to win, and cannot turn down the next throw of the dice, no matter what the stakes. This is a tragic flaw, not unlike those of many other heroes in global epics; the best known of these is Achilles' heel in the *Iliad*, the place where he is most vulnerable. Yudhishthira is so taken with the game that, after losing his worldly goods and his kingdom, he throws in the Pandavas' wife, Draupadi herself, as a stake. Through the use of her wit in a riddle, Draupadi manages to save the Pandava brothers from total ruin. However, they are banished to the forest, and spend twelve years encountering all manner of trials and becoming acquainted with the arts of illusion. In their thirteenth year of exile, they move, in disguise, to the court of King Virata.

As the Kauravas wonder whether their cousins have expired in the forest, the Pandavas emerge and claim their right to the land and the patrimony that the Kauravas have taken in the gambling game. Many armies have gathered around the

Pandavas in support, and they send a final peace-offering to the Kauravas. The Pandavas are inspired by their ally Krishna, emerging at this point in the epic as a king of the neighbouring Vrishni kingdom. Krishna sees his own role as that of mediator. He offers Duryodhana and Arjuna a choice between himself, without arms, and his Vrishni army, filled with tribesmen skilled in war. Arjuna chooses Krishna as a charioteer without arms, and Duryodhana settles for the army.

The Kauravas outnumber the Pandavas by eleven divisions to seven. As with many wars throughout history, both sides scramble to cobble together a last-minute peace. In each attempt at peace, the motives and desires of each character become all the more starkly outlined. Kunti reveals to her son Karna, allied since childhood with the Kauravas, that he is in fact a half-brother of the Pandavas. Duryodhana rejects Krishna, who makes a last-minute diplomatic visit. The Kaurava king Dhritarashtra sends his minister Sanjaya on a similar visit, but Draupadi, who has not forgotten her humiliation in the dice game, persuades the others that war is essential to exact her revenge.

THE *GITA* BEGINS

This atmosphere of resentment and danger sets the tone for the *Gita*. The dramatic tension is only heightened by the powerlessness that the characters feel to stop the inevitable energy of war. Dhritarashtra's personal minister Sanjaya cannot effect peace; in fact, he can only describe the events of the battle to his blind master as they both stand by helplessly. Dhritarashtra begins by asking Sanjaya to narrate to him the events taking place below. Standing beneath them, Arjuna finds his body will not move as he contemplates his relatives on the other side. One by one they are named by Arjuna, just as, only a few verses before, they were named by Duryodhana, who also stands contemplating his cousins in battle array. As readers, we are asked to imagine in detail who is putting their lives at risk, and to come to terms with the full scope of the impending destruction.

Krishna addresses Arjuna's despondence in eighteen Discourses, or teachings. He outlines three options for Arjuna: the *yoga*, or discipline, of *karma*, or action; the *yoga* of *samnyasa*, or renunciation; and the *yoga* of *bhakti*, or devotion – literally, becoming 'a part of' God. As their interaction unfolds, Krishna gradually transforms himself from instructor to divine being. In the tenth and eleventh teachings, Krishna appears in his full, terrifying form as supreme god. He persuades Arjuna to take up arms, as his warrior *dharma* instructs him to do. And Arjuna follows his advice.

The war lasts eighteen days. It involves great individual battles between warriors whom we have come to know, as well as the slow death of Bhishma, the great-uncle of all. The ethics of battle are gradually abandoned by Arjuna, by Bhima and even by Krishna himself. Both sides resort to a series of tricks to undermine the morale of the warriors on the other side: stopping the wheels of their vehicles, forcing them to lay down their weapons and distracting them with grief.

At the end of the battle, Duryodhana takes refuge in a lake, as his powers allow him to do. He emerges only to undergo a brutal battle with the Pandavas, which, in turn, forces a night raid on the Pandavas, where all of the Pandavas' sons, except one grandson, Parikshit, are killed. Even the dying Duryodhana curses the cruelty of this act on the part of his brothers, and the Pandavas avenge themselves on the perpetrators.

At the end, all the Kaurava brothers except three are dead. Yudhishthira is proclaimed king of Hastinapura – a pyrrhic victory at best, in which the cost of war is almost unbearable for all. He reigns unhappily for fifteen years, doing his best to reincorporate Dhritarashtra and Gandhari into the family. Eventually, Dhritarashtra and his wife Gandhari, accompanied by Kunti, go into the forest to practise austerities, only to be burned in a house fire upon their return. Krishna in his human form returns to the western city of Dvaraka to rule over an increasingly disorderly tribe. The Pandavas crown their grandson, Parikshit, as king, and then retire to the Himalayas. Their pilgrimage witnesses the death of all the travellers except

Yudhishthira, who undergoes a test of *dharma* before entering into heaven.

WHAT: THE STRUCTURE AND CONCEPTS OF THE *GITA*

Background

In the last few centuries BCE, the economic, social and historical context in which the *Gita* emerged was as complex and sophisticated as any society today. For many centuries, the Vedas (literally, 'knowledge' of sacred poetic formulae) were the guide for right action, which was sacrifice, or *yajña*. Sacrifice involved the practice of daily, monthly and yearly offerings to many deities, such as Agni, the god of fire, Indra, the warrior god, Vayu, the god of the wind, or Surya, the god of the sun. Sacrifice was understood to be the driving force behind the universe; and if it was not conducted, the sacred order, or *rita*, would be replaced by chaos.

As the civilizations on the Gangetic plain became more settled and urban, the opportunities to remove oneself from society became more possible. The practice of renunciation emerged during the ninth to fourth centuries BCE, and is discussed in texts called the Upanishads. The Upanishads (lit., to 'sit down near') are records of conversations where students and teachers who have retired to the forest explore the nature of reality and how it might be learned through study and meditation. Such study usually involved living in a teacher's house, away from society, and being celibate. One might choose a path of renunciation for a period of studentship, during one's youth, or for one's lifetime, beginning with youth and enduring until old age. One might also choose this path for the end of life, after one has completed one's duties as a householder, raised children and earned a living. The early Vedic compositions are known as *shruti*, or 'that which is heard', and are understood as a kind of revelation. The *Mahabharata* epic in which the Gita occurs, as well as other epics and later literature, is known as *smriti*, 'or that which is remembered'.

In light of this short history, we know that by the time the text of the *Mahabharata* (and therefore the *Gita*) emerged in ancient India as we know it, there were multiple paths to becoming a spiritually advanced person, both through sacrifice and through meditation. Or, to put it in the words of the *Gita*, both action and the renunciation of action were valid means of living a life. In addition, the evidence of the *Mahabharata* tells us that many deities were honoured during this period, some of whom were the older, Vedic deities, and some of whom, such as Krishna, were newly emerging as part of the written record. And inevitably, there were tensions as to which path of life was best: (1) action in sacrifice, or in householdership; (2) renunciation in study, meditation and the pursuit of knowledge; or (3) honouring the deities through devotion.

The Three Strands of the *Gita*

Throughout the centuries, the *Gita* has been understood as containing three basic instructions for how to live according to these three paths: of action (*karmamarga*), of knowledge (*jñanamarga*) and of devotion (*bhaktimarga*). Each has been extolled at various points as the 'central meaning' of the text, and each of them is a compelling form of life, containing resonances, not only in ancient India, but also today. It is this translator's view that, true to its sophisticated nature, the *Gita* places all three in productive tension with each other, and asks its readers and listeners to decide for themselves which path is best.

The path of knowledge involves understanding the categories of the ancient world, and enumerating all possible forms within it. The path of knowledge also involves knowing how we travel from one life to the next, and how we might reduce the endless cycle of suffering that such travel entails. The path of action involves understanding how to connect one's deeds to one's sacred duty, revealed in one's birth and station in life. The path of action also involves a discussion of the path of non-action, or renunciation. (In early India, the path of renunciation was seen as action's opposite – a turning away from the world in order to reduce one's 'footprint' in this life and the next.) Finally, the path of devotion involves an understanding that God, in this case Krishna, stands above all elements and forces in the world. Taking refuge in God is the only form of resolving the inevitable tensions that the worlds of knowledge and action produce.

In respect for this conceptual richness of the *Gita*, I have decided to leave several words untranslated: *samkhya*, *dharma*, *yoga* and *guna*. These ideas are complex in meaning and connotation, yet they are also important structural concepts for reading the *Gita*. If we understand them, we also understand much of early Indian history and thought.

The Path of Knowledge (*jñanamarga)*: *atman* and Brahman

The path of knowledge involves the early Indian teachings of *samkhya* and *yoga*. These teachings were present in the centuries leading up to the composition of the *Gita*. Seeds of these ideas were present in the Upanishads. Particularly important is the idea that Brahman is the elemental force that inspires all things animate and inanimate in the universe. To know Brahman is to understand that one's small self, or *atman*, is at one with the larger forces that quicken the world around us. Hence the well-known Upanishadic equation: *atman* = Brahman. Indeed, some understood the relationship between the *Gita* and the Upanishads to be so close that they understood the *Gita* as a kind of 'later' Upanishad of sorts, in which these kinds of teachings were revealed.

The discussion of *atman* and Brahman is very much present in the *Gita*. *Atman* is understood as a 'self', but not the separate 'self' as one might know it in the West. Rather, *atman* is already connected to all other selves, and the work of the meditating person, the one who is 'restrained', is to understand this inherent interconnectedness. The self moves from life to life in the cycle of birth and death called *samsara*, and it casts off its attributes in each life as it moves on to the next. As *Gita* 2.24 states, the self is 'all-pervading and fixed – unmoving from the beginning'. The self is all-pervading because it is identical with Brahman, the force that inspires all things. Brahman is the ultimate source of *atman*, and the highest place to which the self can aspire. The *Gita* is quick to point out that Brahman encompasses, and is the source of, sacrificial action, and indeed all action.

Brahman and God

Some readers might wonder, 'Is Brahman the same as God?' And the answer is both 'yes' and 'no'. Brahman is the source of all things, and yet we learn from the unfolding of the great dialogue between Arjuna and Krishna that there is more. Throughout the *Gita*, we gradually learn that Krishna is the source of all things, including Brahman. This insight, particularly emphasized in the later Discourses of the *Gita*, leads many of its readers and interpreters to think of the *Gita* as ultimately a theological text, whose main aim is the teaching about God. Krishna speaks of himself as the one who places the embryo of all beings in the 'womb' of Brahman (14.3–4). And in verse 14.27, Krishna argues that he is the 'support' of Brahman.

In the later Discourses of the *Gita*, and especially the Eleventh and Twelfth Discourses, a 'theophany' occurs, an awe-inspiring manifestation of God which dwarfs all other perceptions and ways of thinking. Krishna overwhelms Arjuna with this vision, in which the warrior is both terrified and inspired. Warriors rush like moths into Krishna's mouth, and flames surround him on all sides. Krishna also reassures Arjuna that he is the only one who has seen the full manifestation of God (11.52–3); not even the gods have had the privilege that Arjuna has had. Thus, what started as a companionship between warriors has become a relationship between a devotee and God, in which God manifests a sacred vision given to him alone.

Yoga and *Samkhya*

Yoga is another equally important term that helps us to see the relationship between knowledge, study and the ultimate realities of Brahman and Krishna. *Yoga* is frequently translated as 'discipline' or 'spiritual path'. In Western cultures, it is frequently associated with a regimen of stress-relieving exercise with some spiritual teachings attached. Originally, the term *yoga* derives from the verbal root *yuj*, 'to yoke' or 'to join', and thus, relatedly, to 'engage intensely in something, to follow a discipline'. The idea of 'yoking' has very important connotations: it is a very serious path, a mantle or a harness taken on, as the concrete term 'yoke' implies. *Yoga* almost always involves some kind of meditation or focused concentration. And *yoga* is the path to Brahman.

Yoga is very similar to, and derives from, *samkhya*, a school of philosophy involving the enumeration of all things in the universe and very much a part of the *Gita*'s teachings. In *samkhya*, the world is divided into *purusha*, the animating spirit, gendered masculine, which undergirds all things in the universe, and *prakriti*, the material nature of the created world, gendered feminine. *Purusha* is animated by *prakriti*. In addition, the entire world of *prakriti*, or material nature, possesses three 'qualities', called *guna*s: *sattva*, truth, *rajas*, passion, and *tamas*, darkness. Each entity's way of being in the world is determined by how these qualities are combined and which quality dominates.

Yoga accepts the cosmological view of the universe in *samkhya* thought, and teaches that knowledge of such animating and animated principles is essential to enlightenment. However, *yoga* focuses on meditation in addition to knowledge, and it incorporates a focus on Isha, or the Divine Being, as one of the stages of meditation. When the Indian thinker Patañjali wrote his *Yoga Sutras* around the second century BCE (on the early side of when the *Gita* might possibly have been composed), he conceived of eight stages of *yoga*, involving posture, breathing, mental focus and ultimately the dissolution of the distinction between subject and object. *Yoga* can involve a number of paths, such as *hatha yoga*, cleansing all levels of the body with physically based techniques, *laya yoga*, the dissolution of the self, or *mantra yoga*, the focus on utterance of mantra as a path towards enlightenment.

Many different kinds of *yoga* are spoken about in the *Gita*. A distinction is made in verse 3.3 between the *yoga* of knowledge (*samkhya*) and the *yoga* of action (*karma yoga*). Relatedly, *yoga* is also the discipline of acting without regard for the fruits of action, because one is aware of the true nature of the universe, the eternally transmigrating *atman*, or self, and the importance of adhering to one's true *dharma*, or sacred duty. For this reason, *yoga* is frequently 'joined to insight' (*buddhi*) in the *Gita*'s verses. In verse 2.50, *yoga* is described as skill in, or 'ease in action'. Krishna also describes *yoga* as eternal and ancient, something to abide in for ever as a way of being and wisdom. In its ancient and revered status, *yoga* is also a spiritual path of devotion that was passed down from the royal sages, or *rishi*s, but has become lost to the contemporary world in which the *Mahabharata* war is being fought. Verses 4.2–3 of the *Gita* suggest this idea.

Finally, Krishna hints that *yoga* is a path of devotion to Krishna himself. In verses 6.14–15, Krishna tells Arjuna outright that one who is joined to *yoga*, 'with me as highest', is the one who attains peace. This teaching is an insight that builds slowly through the text that the best *yoga* of action is one that revolves around Krishna as its centre. Thus, while *yoga* tends to mean the particular school of thought and practice described above, in the *Gita* it has many connotations – an ancient secret teaching, a path of disciplined meditation, a path of action joined to insight and a path of devotion to Krishna.

Guna

A word about the term *guna*, or the three qualities of the universe, accepted by both the *samkhya* and the *yoga* systems, is also in order here. As mentioned above, *guna*s are of three types: *sattva, rajas* and *tamas*. In this translation, I have tried to use these terms exactly, including their adjectival forms, 'sattvic', 'rajasic' and 'tamasic'. *Sattva* is more than just its literal meaning of truth, but rather the quality of truth to which one should aspire – filled with light, a form of honest and pure moral conduct. Some have translated *sattva* as 'lucidity'. *Sattva* tends to be associated with the moral ideal for brahmins as teachers and priests. *Rajas*, on the other hand, is the quality of passion, being connected to the fruits of actions and being overjoyed or disappointed at the results of those actions. Just as *sattva* is light (both in terms of the spectrum and in terms of weight), *rajas* tends to be heavy, and associated with struggle. *Rajas* tends to be the quality that warriors are most associated with. Finally, *tamas* is the quality of darkness, and that quality is associated with negative behaviour, greed, laziness and dishonesty. According to the *Gita*, this quality weighs all beings down, and is an impediment on the path of the *yoga* of action, with Krishna at its centre. *Tamas* tends to be associated with the dark and the demonic rather than the divine. Krishna advises all people to strive toward *sattva*, no matter what their station in life.

The *guna*s are part of the material universe and an inevitable part of acting in the world. Since action is an inevitable part of who we are and what we do, part of the task of following the path of *yoga* is to be free of clinging to that material universe, and the *guna*s that constitute it. Krishna explains this idea in verse 2.45. Here it is important to add that while *sattva* is a *guna*, and therefore part of *prakriti*, it is still a positive *guna* which can help one along the path to fulfilment and accomplishment. Frequently such positive traits are described in early Indian texts as 'rafts' or 'temporary goals' which help one along the way. Even though one wants to be free of destructive attachment, one can cling to *sattva* as a positive quality because one can use it in order eventually to attain the larger state of non-clinging.

Action, Non-Action and Acting without Regard for the Fruits

In this translation, 'action' is the translation of the word *karma*. *Karma* is far more complex than simply a single deed, or moment of agency. Rather, it denotes both the pattern of actions in one's life, the ways in which one leads one's life according to one's station in life, and the pattern of action and consequence that keeps us in the cycle of death and rebirth. Most importantly for Western readers, *karma* does *not* mean what it has come to mean in some English slang – simply 'luck' or 'fortune'.

The first time the *Gita* mentions 'action' is in verse 2.43, when Krishna is criticizing those who sacrifice, and know the ancient verses of the Vedas, but do so only for their own reward. Here it might seem as if Krishna is criticizing action per se, and preferring a path of non-action, or renunciation. But this is not the case. Rather, he is arguing that one can and should act in this world, but not to gain reward (2.47). Krishna sees Arjuna faltering, and he shows him a way in which Arjuna could act without clinging to the consequences, or fruits. This is a central message of the *Gita*. Turning to inaction, and clinging to the renunciant path, is equally problematic for Krishna. Inaction, or non-action, is not a solution to the problem of action.

There are several reasons for Krishna's argument. First, the renunciant path is simply another form of action. Second, one can cling to renunciation as destructively as one can cling to the path of action (3.4). By virtue of the nature of the universe, action is present all the time, even when we think we are not acting (3.5). Even without willing it one is made to perform action.

It is important to be clear: the *Gita* is not criticizing non-action, or renunciation, as a way of life. In many parts of the *Gita*, Krishna praises renunciation. Rather, the text is arguing that it is illusory to assume that non-action, or renunciation, is the solution to the dilemmas that face us. In the same way, the *Gita* is not criticizing ritual action per se as a way of life. There are many places in the text where sacrifice and Vedic knowledge per se are praised. Rather, the *Gita* is saying that action without insight, and action while clinging to the fruits, leads us astray. Thus, the resolution for Krishna is to act, but to act with insight about the nature of clinging, and the importance of non-clinging, or letting go of the fruits. For such a wise person, the things that frequently motivate us to act are no longer powerful agents in our lives. For instance, opposites of sensation, such as cold and hot, or feeling, such as hate and love, are experienced as 'the same', because one has let go of the results of either (2.48).

Dharma

Does letting go of the results of action mean that one might act without morality? Not in the least. The *Gita* understands that acting is grounded in *dharma*, or the code of ethics based on one's sacred duty in the universe. One might argue that the *Gita* is entirely about *dharma*. Arjuna asks his teacher and companion Krishna to begin the dialogue, and to teach him the true nature of things, because he cannot face the killing of his own kinsmen (2.7).

Many scholars translate the term *dharma* as 'law' or 'duty'. *Dharma* does incorporate these ideas, and yet has many other important connotations as well. In the early Vedic period *dharma* meant the limit, or boundary, of the sacrificial arena. Yet over time its meaning became more abstract, and it came to mean a limit, or 'organizing principle', for human and even divine behaviour. Yet *dharma* is not simply a principle to be applied; it originates from the sacred order of the universe, and as a result to follow one's *dharma* is to connect with the divine. In the epic of the *Mahabharata*, Arjuna's elder brother, Yudhishthira, is the prince of *dharma*, as the god Dharma, the personification of the principle itself, is his father. Throughout the *Mahabharata*, Yudhishthira is frequently involved in long conversations about *dharma*. But so, too, are his younger brothers, such as Arjuna. The *Gita* is one among many meditations on the nature of the basic question for each individual: 'What is to be done?' or 'How do I fulfil my duty so that I contribute to the overall harmony and right order of the universe?' One way to think of this idea is through the thoughts and words of Martin Luther King, when, in a speech to students in Philadelphia (26 October 1967), he spoke of the street sweeper's relationship to God, perhaps inspired himself by Gandhi's frequent references to street sweepers:

> If it falls to your lot to be a street sweeper, sweep streets like Michelangelo painted pictures, sweep streets like Beethoven composed music, sweep streets like Leontyne Price sings before the Metropolitan Opera. Sweep streets like Shakespeare wrote poetry. Sweep streets so well that all the hosts of heaven and earth will have to pause and say: Here lived a great street sweeper who swept his job well.

There are many *dharma*s to be fulfilled, and certainly one way that we can think of the *Gita*, and the *Mahabharata* as a whole, is a meditation on the conflict between multiple *dharma*s. There is the *dharma* of family roles, whether it be cousin, brother, father or mother (and one should remember here that cousins, in ancient Indian culture as well as in the present day, tend to be understood as 'brothers' rather than the more distant relationship that the English term 'cousin' implies). Thus the heartbreak of Arjuna's dilemma is even deeper, because he is forced to think of the *dharma* of his family role as well as the *dharma* of his work as a warrior. What is more, there is the *dharma* of the honouring of one's elders, especially one's parents and teachers, and Arjuna's great-uncle, Bhishma, as well as his teacher Drona, are on the opposing side. This principle of family *dharma* is behind the dramatic recitation of names in the First Discourse of the *Gita*, when Sanjaya describes to Dhritarashtra whom he 'sees' on the battlefield, and Arjuna understands the intense nature of his relationship to each one of them.

The *dharma* of one's *varna*, or 'station in life', is one of the most important in early India, and Krishna advises Arjuna to follow this *dharma* above all, as long as those actions are devoted to Krishna. These are the *dharma*s of being a brahmin priest; a *kshatriya*, or warrior; a *vaishya*, or merchant; and a *shudra*, or servant. While there are variations on each of the *varna*s within these large four categories, the sacred quality of appropriate behaviour is emphasized in many different ways. Indeed, as verses 1.40–43 state, if one goes outside the laws of *dharma*, the world can become chaotic, and those who break the *dharma* of family and caste are destructive forces. So, too, *dharma* becomes so important that to take on another's *dharma* implies death (3.35).

Krishna ultimately concludes that, as his work is to help Arjuna learn his own *dharma*, he should help him accept the role of a warrior, fighting wrongs that have been done, even by his own family. Krishna speaks such words early on in the text (such as verse 2.31), and repeats them throughout. *Dharma*, then, is not a single meaning, but rather a cluster of meanings, all revolving around our appropriate role in the universe. One might well argue that the *Mahabharata*, with the *Gita* as its primary example, is a meditation on the conflicts that our inevitable multiple *dharma*s introduce.

Bhakti

To resolve many of these conflicts, Krishna repeatedly tells Arjuna throughout the *Gita*, one must turn over one's conflicts and resort to Krishna himself. This is *bhakti*, the path of devotion, which is emphasized so strongly in the final Discourses of the *Gita*, especially after Krishna's theophany. But even before this, Krishna leaves hints to Arjuna. In discussing the role of death and rebirth and the cycle of transmigration, Krishna declares in verse 4.9 that those who are truly devoted to him do not get born again, but go to Krishna himself. Devotion to Krishna is thus partly a function of knowledge, not just 'blind faith' or faith based on emotion alone. In the very next verse, Krishna argues that discipline is crucial for the path of *bhakti* (4.10). And, finally, in 4.11, Krishna articulates that devotion is a mutual endeavour; for if people devote themselves to him, then he in turn will be devoted to them. This idea of 'mutual devotion' is a very important idea throughout classical Indian religions.

Devotion, then, is not simply an emotional approach to God, as we sometimes understand it in contemporary Western culture. *Bhaktimarga* is a path which involves knowledge, discipline and the mutual faithfulness between God and those who resort to God. This idea has inspired readers, chanters and interpreters across many different civilizations to understand its message as a more transcultural interpretation of faith.

WHERE: THE FIELD OF *DHARMA*

Where might the *Mahabharata* war have been fought, if it was indeed a real battle at all? The text places it in Kurukshetra, 'the field of the Kurus'. The contemporary village bearing this name is found north of Delhi in the state of Uttar Pradesh. Many other villages with names similar to those in the *Mahabharata* can be found in this area. However, it is difficult to prove conclusively that these were the same sites. Pottery found in this area called Painted Gray Ware suggests a uniform use of kiln firing, pigment and design, in accordance with a long and consistent pattern of civilization.

Excavations in this area include iron seals, terracotta discs, copper utensils and oblong-shaped ivory dice, also mentioned in the *Mahabharata* in the great dicing scene. Iron objects distinguish this civilization from earlier ones, and include hooks, axes and knives, as well as shafts, arrows and spearheads which could have been used as weapons. Thus, there is archaeological evidence that a civilization existed consistent with that described in the *Mahabharata*. And there is a possibility, if no conclusive evidence, that a large-scale war could have been fought around the ninth century BCE, somewhere in this area. The contemporary village called Kurukshetra now stakes its claim as the original site of the battle and the place of the *Gita* dialogue between Arjuna and Krishna, and it has become a pilgrimage destination among many Hindus. The grounds include a shrine of the *Gita*, which holds as many as three hundred commentaries on the text from different periods in Indian history.

WHEN: THE DATE OF THE *GITA*

Opinions about the date of the *Gita* are as varied as the number of communities who now claim it as their own. Indian and Western scholarly philological communities have come to a rough consensus that the *Bhagavad Gita* was inserted into the larger composition of the *Mahabharata* between the second century BCE and the second century CE. Some argue that the *Gita* was not originally part of the *Mahabharata* but was added to it (there are in fact sixteen sections called 'Gitas' in the entire epic).

It is clear that the author or authors of the *Gita* were familiar with the Upanishads, the earlier 'forest-dwelling' texts mentioned above. Moreover, the *Gita* contains references to many different religious paths, also reflective of an early Indian milieu where schools of Buddhist, Jain and Brahminical systems were competing. Indian thinkers from later centuries, such as Panini and Patañjali, as well as the authors of Buddhist and Jain works, mention Krishna and the events of the Kurukshetra war. In light of the opinions of different scholars, most date the *Gita* to around 150 BCE, a date based on the circumstantial evidence available to us.[3] Some traditional Hindu forms of dating disagree with philological methods, and focus on astrological and astronomical calculations and references within the *Mahabharata* itself to arrive at much earlier possible dates.

The larger question of the manner of composition of the *Gita* is as complex as the dating question. Traditionally, the author of the *Gita* is the same author of the *Mahabharata* itself: the great sage Vyasa, who dictated the epic to Ganesha, the divine scribe. The *Mahabharata* probably existed in oral form, with a great deal of variation, for many centuries before 150 BCE. Singers would travel through different courts and regions, and with their own details and flourishes tell the tale. Interaction between audience and storyteller, as well as the individual creativity of the storyteller, would have been part of the process.[4] And the *Gita* may well have been part of these variations.

WHY: THE INTELLECTUAL AND SOCIAL SIGNIFICANCE OF THE *GITA*

The Early Indian Commentaries

While the *Gita* is located in the sixth book of the *Mahabharata*, the Book of Bhishma, chapters 23–40, it is also a text which can stand alone, with its own independent teaching. As such, it was an object of commentary from the very early stages of Indian history. For many Indian thinkers, writing a commentary on a sacred text was almost as sacred as reading or composing the text itself. A commentator was honouring the original author of the text, as well as creating a 'tradition' which lasted throughout time, in which others could follow. Writing a commentary was a transformative act, in which the author gained merit and spiritual growth.

The *Gita* was no exception to these ideas. The Muslim writer Alberuni commented in the tenth century that the *Mahabharata* was a text sacred to many Indians, and thus the *Gita* must have been a text known to many Hindus at this time. There are more than fifteen ancient Sanskrit commentaries on the *Gita*, and these themselves produced sub-commentaries. In addition, from the tenth century onward, there are partial translations into Telugu, Old Javanese and Persian, and many *Gitasara*s, or 'essences' of the *Gita*, which paraphrase the teachings contained therein into a single 'seed' of thought. However, the texts' multiple emphases have inspired one Indian thinker, T. G. Mainkar, to write that no single commentator has been absolutely faithful to the *Gita*.[5]

The best-known early commentary is that of the philosopher Shankara, born in the late eighth century CE. His work on the *Gita* was one of the cornerstones of his Advaita, or 'non-dual' philosophy that understood all phenomena in the world as illusory, and subordinate to the one, universal animating principle of Brahman. The *Gita*'s main message was this path of knowledge (*jñana*) of Brahman. But other authors disagreed with Shankara, and felt that God's qualities should be understood as real. The best known was Ramanuja, who lived about two centuries later than Shankara. He argued that the path of devotion (*bhakti*), and not knowledge, was more important, and comprised the real force behind the teachings of the *Gita*, particularly the Twelfth and Eighteenth Discourses. Others, such as Madhva (twelfth century CE), taught that both paths of the *Gita* were essential; still others, such as the writer Abhinavagupta, argued for a mystical interpretation of the *Gita* whereby external actions of this world became less necessary as one gained knowledge of Brahman.

The *Gita* in Encounter with the West

The British colonial environment and the rise of the East India Company provided a new stage for the emergence of the *Gita* as a transcultural text.[6] In 1785, the *Gita* made its first appearance in the European context in the translation of a Company merchant, Charles Wilkins, commissioned by Warren Hastings, who saw in the text both wisdom and a means of reconciling Hindu and British sensibilities. The subsequent century saw philosophers, such as Humboldt, comment on the *Gita*'s understanding of *dharma*, and Schlegel's translation into Latin, Abbé Peraud's into French and T. H. Griffiths' into English. The American transcendentalists Emerson and Thoreau found inspiration for their ideas about 'the self' in the *Gita*, and Max Mueller commissioned the Indian author K. K. Telang to translate the text as part of his Sacred Books of the East series. Most famous was Sir Edwin Arnold's poetic rendering of the *Gita*, called 'The Song Celestial'. While Mueller and others understood the *Gita* in comparison to other Indian sacred texts, Arnold and the earlier thinkers understood it as timeless philosophy. In the 1880s, with printing presses in industrial cities producing translations in German, French, English and Latin, the *Gita* was as accessible to the average European as it was to the average Hindu, if not more so.

By the 1890s, the *Gita* had also emerged in India as a national symbol, accessible beyond the Hindu religious experts. Two major ideas placed the *Gita* at the forefront: the idea of India as a motherland and the idea that Krishna was an *avatara*, or incarnation, of Vishnu who re-established the law of *dharma*, or righteous conduct, in the land. Bikram Chandra Chatterji (1836–94) composed an unfinished commentary on the *Gita*, in which Krishna as the ideal man could be part of India's answer to the technological domination and missionizing zeal of colonialism. The leader of the Theosophists, Annie Besant, understood Arjuna as a model for the 'mind unfolding'; she saw his opposing family, the Kauravas, as the lower desires of man, the passion against which we all battle. The Theosophists joined with Bal Gangadhar Tilak (1856–1920) and formed the All-India Home Rule League. While incarcerated, Tilak wrote his commentary on the *Gita*, *Gitarahasya*. For Tilak, Arjuna is initially an unenlightened warrior, but when enlightened he becomes a true warrior, using violent means as necessary; resisters to the colonial regime must function in the same way. For these thinkers, the *Gita* was both a 'universal philosophy' and 'essential Hinduism', proof of India's spiritual superiority to the West, and therefore its need for independence.

For other thinkers of this period, such as the militant-turned-spiritual leader Sri Aurobindo, the *Gita* did not simply teach *dharma* with the good of the nation at heart. Rather, the *Gita* taught *karma*, *bhakti* and *jñana* as a form of practical discipline, or practical *yoga*. The three steps of action, devotion and knowledge form a unified synthesis against which any single verse must be interpreted. Another reformer, Swami Vivekananda, also gave lectures on the *Gita* to Western audiences as his fame grew as a 'translator' of Hinduism in America and Europe. Vivekananda, too, embraced what he saw as the inherent pluralism of the *Gita*, comparing Jesus to Krishna as an emanation of the universal deity. When he spoke to Indian audiences, he emphasized Krishna and Arjuna as 'men of action' who had the energy and insight to reform Hindu society and resist British oppression.

The most important interpreter of the *Gita* for the twentieth century was M. K. Gandhi, who was introduced to the text via the Theosophical Society in London. Gandhi was not a textual interpreter, but a man of moral action whose goal was to take the *Gita*'s principles to heart. He called the *Gita* his 'spiritual dictionary', and used it to give political and spiritual advice as well as to perfect the state of his own soul. In his view, the *Mahabharata* should not be read as a historical text, but rather as a large allegorical teaching in which forces of good and evil battle against each other. Gandhi also understood the events of the *Gita* as a pyrrhic victory, an object lesson in which the cost of the war was too great. Thus, the *Gita* was a teaching about non-violence, not violence. This non-violent essence of the *Gita* was contained in the last twenty verses of the Second Discourse, which describe a person who has achieved control over his inner self. Cold and hot, desire and hatred, even gold and dung, are the same to that person, and he or she exists in a heightened state of mental balance, and does not cling to anything. Such a person could embody *satyagraha*, the force of truth, and so act non-violently in the world. For Gandhi, renunciation, or *samnyasa*, and self-control were far more key to the *Gita* than knowledge or devotion.

Gandhi's use of the *Gita* for personal moral reflection as well as political guidance reflects its social uses during this late colonial period. From the establishment of the Gita Press in the early twentieth century in Gorakpur, the *Gita* became a staple in many different kinds of walks of life. During one period of resistance to colonial rule, anyone with more than one copy of the *Gita* in his possession was considered a terrorist against the state. In a different vein, in 1927 the Gita Press began producing 'Gita Diaries' in which the verses of the text are divided over the whole year in daily meditations.

The Postcolonial *Gita*

In independent India, the *Gita* is now a text that lives between East and West, low-caste and brahmin, rich and poor, secular and sacred. S. V. Radhakrishnan, one of the great philosophers of independent India, still saw the *Gita* as the basis for ethical action in Hinduism and other traditions of the world. So, too,

Vinoba Bhave continued the Gandhian tradition of social reform, based in part on his interpretation of the *Gita* and his ideas of *dana*, or giving.

The most widespread interpretation of the *Gita* in the West was that of Swami Bhaktivedanta, who founded the International Society for Krishna Consciousness (ISKCON). In his teachings, the Swami argued that *bhakti* was the central meaning of the text. Devotion to Krishna alone was its essence. Since its appearance in 1972, *The Bhagavad Gita as It Is* continues to be issued. The *Gita* figures in another spiritual movement that translated into the West – that of Maharishi Mahesh Yogi, who introduced the idea of transcendental meditation (TM). His commentary on the *Gita* appeared in 1967, and in it he argued that the *Gita*'s goal was divine union, 'to raise the consciousness of man to the highest'.

In contemporary India, the *Gita* is thought to be appropriate for children to learn as they are growing up, both in translation into their regional languages as well as in intermediate classes of Sanskrit. Many regional commentaries remain popular, such as those of Jñaneshwari in Maharashtra. One could argue that, in the second millennium, as the regional languages in India were developing their own identities and literatures, the *Gita* became a 'link text' between the Sanskritic traditions and the regional and local traditions. Its relatively simple grammar and its time-honoured place in culture allowed it to be part of everyday life, and not necessarily only an elitist, brahminical text. As such, the *Gita* also functions as a force of social consolidation in urban India – the one set of verse shared in the classroom that every child can recite as part of his or her basic cultural education. It should also be noted, however, that in rural India there are also many Hindus who do not treat the *Gita* as their canonical text.

In America, Europe and Africa, too, the *Gita* has also had a powerful influence among Hindu diaspora communities, and is understood as a foundational guide for life. Most Hindu students in classrooms today have encountered the *Gita* at home. Many of the Hindu temples that decorate the diaspora landscape, especially in urban centres such as London, Atlanta,

Pittsburgh and Birmingham, regularly hold classes on the *Gita*'s message for today. Many such temples also hold *Gita* recitation contests for young students.

Indeed, many of the women who now teach Sanskrit in India are trained first and foremost on the *Gita*; it is understood as a staple of childhood education, with verses passed down in the household from grandmother to mother to daughter, as well as from father to son. Indeed, in my own recent research, one woman mentioned that while her grandmother was illiterate, the old woman still taught her the *Gita* every morning after they had had their morning baths. Transmission of the *Gita* presumes neither literacy nor patriarchy; it is one of the few 'elite' texts that have crossed this particular boundary.

The *Gita* Represented: Artistic Renditions

The precolonial, colonial and postcolonial *Gita* has been represented artistically in a variety of forms. Early medieval manuscripts of the *Mahabharata*, including the *Gita*, are accompanied by illustrations, and go back as early as the tenth century, and probably much earlier. Paintings in the Rajasthani, Moghul and Chola schools of art include 'the great dialogue' in their subjects. The *Gita* inspired the poet and artist William Blake, and several European translations, such as those of Arnold, Burnouf and Tirman, were published with illustrations. The Gita Press established the practice of accompanying *Gita* editions with popular poster art and *Gita* calendars with daily meditations. Since then, several American editions, particularly the *Bhagavad Gita as It Is*, have appeared with Indian poster art. The *Amaracitrakatha*, a comic-book series of several Indian classics, also has produced several Gitas.

The *Gita* has been chanted in temples, towns and private homes probably for as long as it has been a significant sacred text. In both India and the diaspora, cities and towns sponsor *Gita* '*bhajan*' societies – groups which gather regularly to chant the *Gita*. So too, musical renditions of the *Gita* abound and have been adapted to different musical media as they develop.

Records and tapes were issued from Hindu communities such as the Swami Chinmaya, Ramakrishna and Vasvani Missions in the 1960s and 1970s, which then emerged as CDs in the 1980s and interactive-computer-based websites by the mid-1990s onward.

European composers such as E. Tremisot and Dvan Hinloopen Laberton have composed choral and instrumental works based on the *Gita*.[7] T. S. Eliot's poetry may well have been influenced by his reading of the *Gita*; and, most recently in the West, Philip Glass's contemporary opera *Satyagraha* features verses of the *Gita* alongside a portrayal of the life of Gandhi. The *Gita* has provided inspiration for 'fusion' music in the late twentieth and early twenty-first centuries, a style which combines Western and Asian rhythms. The 2001 movie *Bagger Vance* used the *Gita* as one of its models for both plot and character. And as recently as 2003 an American jazz group, Bela Fleck and the Flecktones, released a CD, *Left of Cool*, with a track called 'Arjuna's Sojourn'.

Gita dramas and stage adaptations have also been on record since at least the 1920s, and probably much earlier. Local presses in particular have prepared renditions for children and rural women. Since 1938 the Gita Press outreach organization, the Sri Gita Pariksha Samiti, has annual public examinations on the *Gita*, as well as recitation contests in which memorized knowledge of the *Gita* is essential.

In addition, there is a long tradition of the *Gita* 'performed' in everyday life. Its *shloka*s, or metrical verses, are part of the world in which many Hindus live, and thus they act as a kind of resource for commentary on everyday situations. In impromptu performances, in private conversations, as well as in informal writing, people quote the *Gita* as a way of thinking about the situation that faces them. In my own fieldwork, I found that this kind of proverbial utterance of verses from the *Gita* was common – whether it was a woman commenting on her duty to her parents, or a professor thinking about why he was reading a particular section of the *Mahabharata*, or an older child trying to teach a younger one about discipline. These utterances work like proverbs, where they remind the participants in a discussion of a larger principle. Such utterances also help to link the everyday world with the more sacred world.

WHY? READING AND TRANSLATING THE *GITA* IN THE TWENTY-FIRST CENTURY

This translation stands on the shoulders of many preceding giants. Yet the questions of readers in the twenty-first century are not the same as last century, when India won its independence. India and the *Gita* now occupy a place on the global technological and economic stage. 'Hindu' readers are not simply Indian readers, but also American, British, Kenyan, Trinidadian, Canadian and South American readers, just to name a few. Students within diaspora settings do not go about their lives with a Hindu culture around them; frequently, the *Gita* is one of their few vehicles for learning Hindu perspectives. And non-Hindu students who come to the *Gita* for the first time may have greater knowledge of India than previously. Most students are also more aware of multicultural issues within their own immediate environments. Frequently, students' questions are postcolonial ones – about creating identity in new situations, about moving across cultures to find a compelling new set of ideas, about cultural and ethnic ownership, about the possibility of universal values, and so on. And with all of these questions, these students must still 'share' this text, whether it comes from their culture or was translated into it.

In a sense, this postcolonial audience is more likely to be in sympathy with Tejasvini Niranjana's view of translation, where readers are more aware of multiple accounts of both texts and translation practices, of 'resistant' translations, of bilingual translators who challenge earlier Western versions through retranslation. These readers would be engaged by the question of translation as both an aesthetic *and* a social act; the text as both an aesthetic *and* a social document. Indeed, contemporary readers, whatever their location, understand that the two cannot be easily extricated.[8]

With this new readership in mind, this translation's focus is on straightforward language, so that as many readers as possible, from as many cultures as possible, can 'imagine themselves in the text'. Relatedly, except where specific reference to the male gender is intended, this translation is also gender-neutral. If the *Gita* is indeed a global text, then Krishna can be understood as speaking for and about all of humanity. Because I emphasize accessibility as well as accuracy, my hope is that both the sophistication and simplicity of the text can shine through.

NOTES

1. 'Bhagavad Gita' literally means 'Song of the Blessed One' or 'Song of God'. In most contexts, the *Gita* is a shorthand way of referring to the larger text, the *Bhagavad Gita*, and I follow that custom here. While there are other Gitas, or songs, in the *Mahabharata* and elsewhere in ancient Indian literature, most would understand *Gita* to refer to this well-known text.
2. There have been more than 3,000 articles written on the *Gita* in the past 200 years. Studies on most of the major concepts, which will 'point' the reader in further directions of study, are given in subsequent notes. For a general bibliography, see R. J. Venkateswaran, *Dictionary of Bhagavad Gita* (New Delhi: Sterling Publishers, 1991), and Suryakumari Dwarakadas and C. S. Sundaram, *Bhagavadgītā Bibliography* (Chennai: Kuppuswami Sastri Research Institute, 2000). Readers may also consult issues of the *Journal of Studies in the Bhagavadgita*, and Jagdish Chender Kapoor, *Bhagavad Gītā: An International Bibliography of 1785–1979 Imprints* (New York: Garland Publishers, 1983).
3. There are more than fifty recent articles discussing this issue of dating. For an accessible summary, see the cautious note in Robert N. Minor, *Bhagavad Gītā: An Exegetical Commentary* (New Delhi: Heritage Books, 1982), pp. xliii–li. Also see the discussion of the *Mahabharata*'s composition in James L. Fitzgerald's review of Alfred Hiltebeitel, *Rethinking the Mahābhārata: A Reader's Guide to the Education of the Dharma King* (Chicago: University of Chicago Press, 2001): 'The Many Voices

of the Mahābhārata', *Journal of the American Oriental Society*, 124 (2003), 803–18.

4. V. S. Sukthankar, 'Critical Studies in the MBh', in *Sukthankar Memorial Edition*, vol. 1 (Bombay: Karnatak Publishing House, 1944), 1–12.

5. T. G. Mainkar, *A Comparative Study of the Commentaries on the Bhagavadgītā* (Delhi: Motilal Banarsidass, 1969), 65; Arvind Sharma, *The Hindu Gītā: Ancient and Classical Interpretations of the Bhagavadgītā* (London: Duckworth, 1986).

6. Among the many helpful general works on this topic, see Eric J. Sharpe, *The Universal Gītā: Western Images of the Bhagavad Gītā. A Bicentenary Survey* (LaSalle, Ill.: Open Court, 1985); Robert N. Minor (ed.), *Modern Indian Interpreters of the Bhagavadgītā* (New York: State University of New York Press, 1986); P. M. Thomas, *20th Century Interpretations of Bhagavadgita: Tilak, Gandhi and Aurobindo* (Delhi: ISPCK, 1987).

7. See Winand M. Callewaert and Shilanand Hemraj, *Bhagavadgītānuvāda: A Study in Transcultural Translation* (Ranchi: Satya Bharati Publications, 1982), 45–8.

8. Tejasvini Niranjana, *Siting Translation: History, Post-Structuralism, and the Colonial Context* (Berkeley: University of California Press, 1992); for a discussion of postcolonial issues of translation, see esp. pp. 37, 50, 115–19.

Note on the Translation

I have tried to negotiate between the simplicity and accuracy of the Sanskrit language and the poetic, philosophical and religious vision which the *Gita* expresses. With a more diverse audience in mind, it is important to emphasize the dialogical nature of the *Gita*; such verbal exchange is a form of literary and artistic and even philosophical expression in many different cultures. Thus it seemed best to translate each section, called *adhyaya* in Sanskrit, as 'Discourse'. While *adhyaya* is frequently translated as 'chapter', it can also mean a 'teaching' or 'instruction' that occurs between a teacher and a student. 'Discourse' seemed most appropriate because, in addition to delineating a 'section' or 'part' of a text, it implies a kind of conversation about a subject matter, as well as a teaching.

I have opted for poetry over prose, and have tried to make every verse a poem in its own right, creating new associative possibilities in the mind of the reader. In addition, I have opted for eight-line rather than four-line verses, because first-time readers of the *Gita* might have an easier time if they encounter a single concept or image on each line, rather than several new concepts or images on each line. While I think it would sound somewhat contrived to the modern ear to mirror the strict metrical *anushthubh* or *trishthubh* metres of the Sanskrit, I also did not want to work entirely in free verse without restrictions. My query in translating was: What would be the contemporary cultural equivalent of the easygoing and flexible *shloka* in ancient India? And my answer was something like free verse, with a maximum number of eight syllables per line (and frequently far fewer), and a set number of eight lines. In this way, directness of imagery and brevity of expression are the means to preserve the compelling nature of the mythological subjects being treated in the poem. My intention here is not to 'mysticize' the *Gita*, and render it overly poetic in a way which lends itself too much to aesthetic or mystical concerns. In making each verse like a poem, I am aiming to reflect the 'proverbial' or 'aphoristic' nature of the text, in which *shloka*s are selected and quoted to comment on other texts, or on everyday situations.

Second, my intention has been to focus on the simple poetic properties of the Sanskrit language. With all of the complexity of the theological, philosophical and sacrificial worlds during the post-Vedic period in which the *Gita* was probably composed, the text also utilizes the physical image. None of the older, more concrete resonances of the early Vedic world were replaced, but rather they were 'expanded upon' with new, more abstract imagery – hence the oscillation between philosophy and poetry.

In this spirit, whenever possible, I have tried to give the flavour of a Sanskrit compound in all of its poetic specificity. For example, in verse 11.29 the reader encounters the famous image of the warriors moving into Krishna's mouth like moths into a flame. Here, the word for moth is *patanga* (*patam* + *ga*), the 'flying-goer'. One could simply translate as 'moth', but the poetic properties of the word for moth – 'a flying-goer' – would be lost. And the larger image, not simply of moths moving into the mouth, but also of the speed of rushing in to be burned, should be preserved. So, I have translated, 'moths that fly to their full . . .'

Third, I have also chosen to translate the epithets that Arjuna and Krishna use for each other within their conversation, such as 'Scorcher of the Enemy', or 'Mover of Men'. Many scholars assume that these epithets are inserted for metrical purposes. However, it is my view that the use of epithets gives the *Gita* a unique richness and texture. Indeed, epithets function like nicknames in the *Gita*, where Krishna and Arjuna engage in a kind of ironic exchange on the subject at hand. I have provided a list of epithets for both Krishna and Arjuna to make the text accessible and enjoyable for the first-time reader.

In addition, particularly in the First Discourse, many different warriors from both Kaurava and Pandava sides of the war are named. In cases where the name of a warrior has particularly rich meaning, for the reader's enjoyment I use the original Sanskrit name *and* translate that name in the verse itself. I also do this with the names of the conch-shell horns that are blown by the warriors.

It is my hope that these small decisions in translation and poetic construction will make for pleasurable reading. The challenge of the *Gita* should be in the ideas of the text, and yet readers should also be able to take delight in the aesthetics and imagery contained within its language. And so the *samvada*, both internal and external, should continue.

NOTE ON SANSKRIT PRONUNCIATION AND ENGLISH RENDERING

For accessibility for the first-time reader, Sanskrit terms are not written with diacritical markings in this translation, but in Anglicized form. Sanskrit has long vowels, as well as retroflex (also called 'cerebral') consonants (pronounced with the tongue at the roof of the mouth) and dental consonants (pronounced with the tongue near the teeth). These features can only be roughly reproduced in the Anglicized forms of the words. For a full guide to Sanskrit pronunciation, see Sally J. Sutherland and Robert P. Goldman's *Devavāṇīpraveśikā: An Introduction to the Sanskrit Language*, 3rd edition (Berkeley: Center for South Asian Studies, 1999).

Most Sanskrit consonants are pronounced like their English counterparts. Sanskrit 'g' is always pronounced hard, as in 'gull'. And Sanskrit 'c' is always pronounced like the 'ch' in English '*ch*air'. Those consonants spelled with 'h' after them (kh, gh, ch, jh, th, dh, ph, bh), such as the 'dh' in 'Dhritarashtra', are called 'aspirated' consonants. They are pronounced with a short burst of air right after the consonant: the difference between 'red' and 're*dh*ead'. 'Bh' is aspirated as one would the word 'clu*bh*ouse' and 'ph' is aspirated as one would the word 'flo*ph*ouse'. The retroflex 's' is pronounced like the 'sh' in English 'fi*sh*', with the tongue more on the roof of the mouth. The aspirated 's' is pronounced like the 's' in English '*sh*ine'. Both sounds are rendered as 'sh' in this translation.

Sanskrit short 'a' is pronounced like the 'u' in English 'but'. Short 'i' is pronounced as one would the 'i' in English 'bit'. Short 'u' is pronounced as one would the 'u' in English 'put'. Long 'ā' is pronounced as the 'a' in English 'b*a*r'. Long 'ī' is pronounced like the 'ee' in English 'see'. Long 'ū' is pronounced like the 'oo' in English 'moo'. The diphthong 'e' is pronounced like the 'ay' in English 'st*ay*'. The diphthong 'o' is pronounced like the 'o' in English 'mope'. The diphthong 'ai' is pronounced like the 'i' in English 'n*i*gh'. The diphthong 'au' is pronounced like the 'ou' in English 'm*ou*nd'.

When pronouncing Sanskrit words, the accent goes on the 'heavy' syllable. Heavy syllables are those with a long simple vowel (ā, ī, ū), a Sanskrit diphthong (e, i, ai, au) or a short vowel followed by more than one consonant. Thus, to take a simple example, the word 'Krishna' would have the accent on the first syllable.

Further Reading

CRITICISM AND HISTORICAL BACKGROUND

Agarwal, Satya P., *The Social Role of the Gita* (New Delhi: Jainendra Press, 1993).

——, 'Lokasamgraha and Ahimsa in the Bhagavad Gita', *Journal of Dharma*, 16 (July–Sept. 1991), 255–68.

Aiyar, Parameswara, 'Imitations of the Bhagavad Gita and Later Gita Literature', in Haridasa Bhattacaryya (ed.), *The Cultural Heritage of India*, 2nd edn. (Calcutta: Ramakrishna Mission Institute of Culture, 1962).

Apte, K. V., 'Contradictions in the Bhagavadgītā', *Journal of the Asiatic Society of Bombay*, NS 39–40 (1964–5), 104–24.

Arapura, John G., 'Ahimsa and Ecology', *Journal of Dharma*, 16 (July–Sept. 1991), 197–301.

Armstrong, A. H., and Ravindra, R., 'The Dimensions of the Self: Buddhi in the Bhagavad-Gītā and Psyche in Plotinus', *Religious Studies*, 15 (Sept. 1979), 327–42.

Atkinson, D., 'The Gita and Gandhi's Moral Vision', in Braj M. Sinha (ed.), *The Contemporary Essays on the Bhagavad Gita* (New Delhi: Siddharth Publications, 1995).

Barborka, Geoffrey A., *The Pearl of the Orient: The Message of the Bhagavad-Gītā for the Western World* (Wheaton, Ill.: Theosophical Pub. House, 1968).

Bazaz, Prem Nath, *The Role of Bhagavad Gita in Indian History* (New Delhi: Sterling Publishers, 1975).

Belvalkar, S. K., 'The Bhagavad-gītā: A General Study of its

History and Character', in Haridasa Bhattacariyya (ed.), *The Cultural Heritage of India*, 2nd edn. (Calcutta: Ramakrishna Mission Institute of Culture, 1962), vol. 2, pp. 136–7.

——, 'The BG Riddle Unriddled', in *Annals of the Bandharkar Oriental Research Institute*, 19 (1938–9), 335–48.

Berg, Richard A., 'An Ethical Analysis of the Bhagavad Gita', in Braj M. Sinha (ed.), *The Contemporary Essays on the Bhagavad Gita* (New Delhi: Siddharth Publications, 1995), 15–35.

——, 'Theories of Action in the Bhagavad Gita', in Braj M. Sinha (ed.), *The Contemporary Essays on the Bhagavad Gita* (New Delhi: Siddharth Publications, 1995), 36–51.

——, 'The Bhagavad-Gītā on War: The Argument from Literature', *Journal of Studies in the Bhagavadgītā*, 5–7 (1985–7), 25–35.

Besant, Annie Wood, *Hints on the Study of the Bhagavad-Gita: Four Lectures Delivered at the Thirtieth Anniversary Meeting of the Theosophical Society at Adyar, Madras, December, 1905* (Benares: Theosophical Publishing Society, 1908).

Bhagwat, Rajaram Shastri, *Vividhajnanavistara*, no. 7 (1906), 273–82.

Bilimoria, Purushottama, 'R. C. Zaehner's Treatment of the Bhagavad Gītā', *Journal of Studies in the Bhagavadgītā*, 3 (1983), 87–111.

Bolle, K., 'Gandhi's Interpretation of the Bhagavad Gītā', in John Hick and Lamont C. Hempel (eds.), *Gandhi's Significance for Today* (New York: St Martin's Press, 1989), 137–51.

Brink, H. W. van den, 'Het gedenken: Een studie over de yoga in de Bhagavad-Gita met enkele vergelijkende bijbelse aantekeningen', *Nederlands Theologisch Tijdschrift*, 16 (April 1962), 241–56.

Callewaert, Winand M., , 'A "Dynamic Equivalence Translation" of the Bhagavad Gītā', *Journal of Dharma*, 5 (1980), 52–63.

——, and Shilanand, Hemraj, *Bhagavadgītānuvāda: A Study in Transcultural Translation* (Ranchi: Satya Bharati Publications, 1982).

Cenkner, William, 'A New Understanding of the Bhagavad Gītā: Trinitarian Evil', in William Cenkner (ed.), *Evil and the Response of World Religion* (St Paul, Minn.: Paragon House, 1997).

Charpentier, G., 'Some Remarks on the Bhagavadgītā', *Indian Antiquary*, 59 (May 1930), 80–130.

Chattopadhyaya, R. K., 'The Bhagavadgītā and the Vedas', *Calcutta Review*, series 3, no. 161 (Nov. 1961), 190–98.

Dandekar, R. N., 'Hinduism and the Bhagavadgītā: A Fresh Approach', *Journal of the Oriental Institute*, 3 (March 1963), 232–7.

Davis, Roy Eugene, *The Eternal Way: The Inner Meaning of the Bhagavad Gita* (Lakemont, Ga.: CSA Press, Publishers Center for Spiritual Awareness, 1996).

De Nicolás, Antonio T., *Avatāra: The Humanization of Philosophy through the Bhagavad Gītā*, with prologue by Raimundo Panikkar (New York: N. Hayes, 1976).

De Smet, Richard, 'The Integration Doctrine of God of the Bhagavad Gita', in Claetus M. Vadakkekara (ed.), *Prayer and Contemplation* (Bangalore, India: Asirvanam Benedictine Monastery, 1980), 139–57.

——, 'A Copernican Reversal: The Gitakara's Reformulation of Karma', *Philosophy East and West*, 27 (Jan. 1977), 53–6.

Deussen, Paul, *Der Gesang des Heiligen: Eine philosophische Episode des Mahābhāratam* (Leipzig: F. A. Brockhaus, 1911).

Dhar, Mohini Mohan, 'Classical Patterns of Hindu Salvation', *Studia Missionalia*, 29 (1980), 209–71.

——, 'Philosophy of Religion according to the Bhagavad-gītā', in Pontificia Università Salesiana Facoltà di Filosofia (ed.), *Religione, ateismo e filosofia: Scritti in onore del Prof Vincenzo Miano nel suo 70imo compleanno* (Rome: Libreria Ateneo Salesiano, 1980), 37–45.

——, 'Hindu Morality', *Studia Missionalia*, 27 (1978), 217–55.

Divanji, P. C., '*Ātman* and the Terms Allied to it in the *Bhagavadgītā*', *Journal of the Oriental Institute*, 2 (Dec. 1961), 161–4.

——, '"Brahman" and the Terms Allied to it in the Bhagavadgita', *Journal of the Oriental Institute* (June 1959), 367–77.

Easwaran, Eknath, *Bhagavad Gita for Daily Living: Chapters 1 Through 6* (Berkeley: Blue Mountain Center of Meditation, 1975).

Eder, Milton, 'Cultural Literacy and Indian Civilizational Studies: The Bhagavad-Gītā in the Classroom', *Journal of Vaiṣṇava Studies*, 3 (Spring 1995), 143–59.

Edgerton, Franklin, 'On Some Translations and Methods of Interpretation of the Gītā', in *The Bhagavad Gītā or Song of the Blessed One* (Chicago: Open Court, 1925).

——, 'The Meaning of Saṁkhya and Yoga', *American Journal of Philology*, 14/1 (1924), 37–46.

Feuerstein, Georg, *The Bhagavad gītā: Its Philosophy and Cultural Setting* (Wheaton, Ill.: Theosophical Pub. House, 1983 [1974]).

——, *Introduction to the Bhagavadgītā* (London: Rider, 1974).

Fingarette, Herbert, 'Action and Suffering in the Bhagavad Gita', *Philosophy East and West*, 34 (Oct. 1984), 357–69.

Forrest, Robert W. E., 'Theophany in Job and the Bhagavad-Gita', *Journal of Studies in the Bhagavadgītā*, 2 (1982), 25–43.

Garbe, Richard, *Die Bhagavadgītā aus dem Sanskrit ubersetzt mit einer Einleitung über ihre ursprungliche Gestalt, ihre Lehren und ihr Alter*, 2nd edn. (Leipzig: H. Haessel Verlag, 1921).

Garg, R. K., 'Gita-sadhana', *Sevartham*, 19 (1994), 83–99.

——, 'The Gita-Principle of Detached Activism', *Prabuddha Bharata*, 74 (July 1969), 310–14.

Gopalan, S., 'The Concept of Duty in the Bhagavad-Gītā: An Analysis', *Journal of Studies in the Bhagavadgītā*, 5–7 (1985–7), 1–13.

Griffiths, Bede, *River of Compassion: A Christian Commentary of the Bhagavad Gītā* (New York: Continuum, 1995).

——, 'The Advaitic Experience and the Personal God in the Upanishads and the Bhagavad Gita', in Mayeul de Druille (ed.), *Christian Spirituality for India: A Symposium on*

Patristic and Indian Spirituality (Bangalore, India: Asirvanam Benedictine Monastery, 1978), 71–86.

Harris, I., 'The Gita and Vinoba Bhave's Conception of Sarvodaya', in Braj M. Sinha (ed.), *The Contemporary Essays on the Bhagavad Gita* (New Delhi: Siddharth Publications, 1995).

Hegel, Georg Wilhelm Friedrich, *On the Episode of the Mahābhārata Known by the Name Bhagavad-Gītā by Wilhelm von Humboldt*, ed. and trans. Herbert Herring (New Delhi: Indian Council of Philosophical Research, distributed by Munshiram Manoharlal Publishers, 1995).

Herman, A. L., 'Ethical Theory in the Bhagavad Gītā: Theological Attitude Liberationism and Its Implications', *Journal of Vaiṣṇava Studies*, 3 (Spring 1995), 47–69.

——, 'Free Will and Compulsion in [Bhagavad Gītā] 18:14, 59, 61', *Journal of Studies in the Bhagavadgītā*, 1 (1981), 61–99.

Hijiya, James A., 'The "Gītā" of J. Robert Oppenheimer', *Proceedings of the American Philosophical Society*, 144/2 (June 2000), 123–67.

Huber, Friedrich, 'The Relevance of the Bhagavad Gītā according to Paul David Devanandan', *Religion and Society*, 34 (March 1987), 53–65.

Hudson, Dennis, 'Arjuna's Sin: Thoughts on the Bhagavad-gītā in its Epic Context', *Journal of Vaiṣṇava Studies*, 4 (Summer 1996), 65–84.

Jacobi, Hermann, 'Weiteres zum Bhagavadgītā Problem', *Deutsche Literaturzeitung*, 43 (April 1922), 266–73.

——, 'Die Bhagavad Gītā', *Deutsche Literaturzeitung*, 42 (Dec. 1921), 715–24.

——, 'Über die Einfügung der Bhagavadgītā im Mahābhārata', *Zeitschrift der Deutschen Morgenländischen Gesellschaft*, 72 (1910), 323–7.

James, Gene, 'Avatara and Incarnation', *Dialogue & Alliance*, 1 (Summer 1987), 3–92.

Jordens, J. T. F., 'Bhagavadgītā: Karma Exorcised', *Millawa-Milla: The Australian Bulletin of Comparative Religion*, 4 (1964), 22–30.

Kapferer, Roland, 'Contradiction and the Logic of Conversion in the Bhagavad-Gītā', *Journal of Studies in the Bhagavadgītā*, 5–7 (1985–7), 127–37.

Kasimow, Harold, 'A Jewish Encounter with the Bhagavad Gītā', *Journal of Vaiṣṇava Studies*, 3 (Spring 1995), 33–45.

Khair, G. S., *The Quest for the Original Gita* (Bombay: Somaiya Publications, 1969).

Kilbe, M. V., 'An Internal Evidence as Regards the Age of the BG', *Annals of the Bhandharkar Oriental Research Institute*, 24 (1943), 99–100.

Killingley, Siew Yue, 'Time, Action, Incarnation: Shades of the Bhagavad-Gītā in the Poetry of T. S. Eliot', *Literature and Theology*, 4 (March 1990), 50–71.

King, Ursula, 'Iconographic Reflections in the Religious and Secular Importance of the Bhagavad-Gītā within Image World of Modern Hinduism', *Journal of Studies in the Bhagavadgita*, 5–7 (1985–7), 161–88.

——, 'The Iconography of the Bhagavad Gītā', *Journal of Dharma*, 7 (April–June 1982), 146–63.

——, 'Who is the Ideal Karmayogin: The Meaning of a Hindu Religious Symbol', *Religion*, 10 (Spring 1980), 41–59.

Kosambi, D. D., 'Social and Economic Aspects of the Bhagavad Gītā', *Journal of the Economic and Social History of the Orient*, 4/2 (Aug. 1961), 198–224.

Kripananda, Swami, *Jñaneshwar's Gita: A Rendering of the Jñaneshwari* (Albany, NY: State University of New York Press, 1989).

Krishnamoorthy, K., 'The Gita Idea of *Svadharma*', *Aryan Path*, 36/2 (Feb. 1965), 64–72.

Lamotte, F., *Notes sur le Bhagavadgītā* (Paris: Geuther, 1929).

Larson, Gerald James, 'The Song Celestial: Two Centuries of the Bhagavad Gītā in English', *Journal of Studies in the Bhagavadgītā*, 3 (1983), 1–55.

——, 'Bhagavad Gītā as Cross-Cultural Process: Toward an Analysis of the Social Locations of a Religious Text', *Journal of the American Academy of Religion*, 43/4 (Dec. 1975), 651–69.

Loasby, Roland E., 'The Challenge of the Bhagavad-Gita:

Krishna and the Bhakti-Marga', *Andrews University Seminary Studies*, 2 (1964), 79–96.

McLean, Andrew, 'Emerson's Brahma as an Expression of Brahman', *New England Quarterly*, 42/1 (March 1969), 115–22.

Malinar, Angelika, *Rājavidyā: Das königliche Wissen um Herrschaft und Verzicht. Studien zur Bhagavadgītā* (Wiesbaden: Otto Harrassowitz, 1996).

——, 'The Bhagavadgītā in the Mahābhārata TV Serial: Domestic Drama and Dharmic Solutions', *Representing Hinduism* (1995), 442–67.

Mather, D. C., 'The Doctrine of Nishkāma Karma: An Alternative Interpretation', *Quest* (Bombay), 42 (July 1964), 23–5.

Mehta, Rohit, *From Mind to Super-mind: A Commentary on the Bhagavad Gita* (Bombay: Manaktalas, 1966).

Miller, Barbara Stoler, 'Why did Henry David Thoreau Take the Bhagavad-Gita to Walden Pond?', *Parabola*, 12/1 (Spring 1987), 58–63.

Minor, Robert N., 'Krishna and the Ethics of the Bhagavadgītā', in Braj M. Sinha (ed.), *The Contemporary Essays on the Bhagavad Gita* (New Delhi: Siddharth Publications, 1995).

——, *Bhagavad-Gītā: An Exegetical Commentary* (New Delhi: Heritage Books, 1982).

——, 'The Bhagavad-Gītā and Modern Scholarship: An Appraisal of Introductory Conclusions', *Journal of Studies in the Bhagavadgītā*, 1 (1981), 29–60.

——, 'The Gītā's Way as the Only Way', *Philosophy East and West*, 30/3 (1980), 339–54.

Mishra, G. S. P., 'Non-Attachment in Buddhist Texts and the Gītā', *Quest* (Bombay), 45 (April 1965), 49–51.

Mishra, Vijay C., 'Another Stubborn Structure: The Gītā as a Literary Text', *Journal of Studies in the Bhagavadgītā*, 2 (1982), 89–105.

Modi, P. M., 'Twofold Conception of Reality in Bhagavadgītā, Adhyayas I–VI', *Journal of the Maharaja Sayajiro University of Baroda*, 17 (April 1968), 159–65.

——, '"Prakriti" in the Bhagavadgita (with Special Reference to the Saddadvaita Philosophy', *Indian Philosophy and Culture*, 9/3 (Sept. 1960), 39–43.

Moffitt, John, 'Bhagavad Gītā as Way-Shower to the Transcendental', *Theological Studies*, 38 (June 1977), 316–31.

Mumme, P., 'Haunted by Śāṅkara's Ghost: The Śrīvaiṣṇava Interpretation of Bhagavad Gītā 18:66', in Jeffrey R. Timm (ed.), *Texts in Context: Traditional Hermeneutics in South Asia* (Albany, NY: State University of New York Press, 1992), 69–84.

Mundschenck, Paul, 'The Psychology of the Bhagavad-Gītā: Non-Attachment in the Modern World', *Journal of Studies in the Bhagavadgītā*, 5–7 (1985–7), 14–24.

Murdoch, John, *Philosophic Hinduism: The Upanishads, Darsanas, and Bhagavad Gita* (Madras: The Christian Literature Society, 1893).

Nagarajan, S., 'Arnold and the *Bhagavad Gita*: A Reinterpretation of *Empedocles on Etna*', *Comparative Literature*, 12/4 (Autumn 1960), 335–47.

Nayar, Nancy Ann, 'The Bhagavad Gītā and Śrīvaiṣṇavism: Multilevel Contextualization of an Ancient Hindu Text', *Journal of Vaiṣṇava Studies*, 3 (Spring 1995), 115–41.

Nelson, V. Kanagu, 'Bhagavad Gita and Counselling', *Arasaradi Journal of Theological Reflection*, 8 (1995), 98–105.

O'Connell, Joseph T., 'Karma in the Bhagavad-Gītā: Caitanya Vaiṣṇava Views', *Journal of Vaiṣṇava Studies*, 3 (Spring 1995), 91–107.

——, 'Caitanya's Followers and the Bhagavad-Gītā: A Case Study in Bhakti and the Secular', in Bardwell Smith (ed.), *Hinduism: New Essays in the History of Religions* (Leiden: Brill, 1976), 33–52.

Oldenberg, Hermann, 'Die Bemerkungen zur Bhagavadgītā', *Nachrichten von der Königlichen Gesellschaft der Wissenschaften zu Göttigen* (1919), 328–38.

Olivelle, Patrick, 'The Concept of God in the Bhagavad Gītā', *International Philosophical Quarterly*, 4/4 (Dec. 1964), 524–53.

Oltramare, Paul, 'La Bhagavadgītā: partie integrante du

Mahābhārata', *Revue de l'Histoire des Religions*, 97 (1968), 161–85.

Otto, Rudolf, *Die Lehr-Traktate der Bhagavad-gītā* (Tübingen: Mohr, 1935).

——, *Die Urgestalt der Bhagavad-gītā* (Tübingen: Mohr, 1934).

Painadath, Sebastian, 'The Integrated Spriritualitу of the Bhagavad Gita – An Insight for Christians: A Contribution to the Hindu-Christian Dialogue', *Journal of Ecumenical Studies*, 39 (Summer–Fall 2002), 305–24.

Pappu, S. S. Rama Rao, 'Detachment and Moral Agency in the Bhagavad Gita', in id. (ed.), *Perspectives on Vedānta: Essays in Honor of Professor P. T. Raju* (Leiden: E. J. Brill, 1988), 148–57.

Parrinder, E. Geoffrey, *The Significance of the Bhagavad-Gītā for Christian Theology* (London: Dr Williams's Trust, 1968).

Parthasarathy, K. E., 'The Philosophy of Nishkāma Karma in the *Bhagadvad-Gītā*', *Aryan Path*, 38/4 (1967), 160–64.

Pathak, Sushil Madhava, 'The Bhagavad-Gītā and Its Evaluation in Modern Times', *Journal of Studies in the Bhagavad-gītā*, 8–9 (1988–9), 11–24.

Patrapankal, Joseph, 'Hermeneutics', *Journal of Dharma*, 5 (Jan.–March 1980), 1–22.

Prasad, P. S. K., *Bhagavad Gita Explained to the Modern Man* (Hyderabad: K. Pandrangi, 2001).

Prithipaul, K., 'An Appraisal of Hegel's Criticism of the Bhagavad Gita and Hindu Spirituality', in Braj M. Sinha (ed.), *The Contemporary Essays on the Bhagavad Gita* (New Delhi: Siddharth Publications, 1995), 156–85.

Quéguiner, Maurice, 'Die Bhagavad-Gītā und der Krieg', *Kairos*, 2/4 (1960), 233–9.

Raghavan, V., 'Greater Gītā', *Journal of Oriental Research Madras*, 12/1 (1942/43), 86–122.

Rangacarya, M., *The Hindu Philosophy of Conduct; being lectures on the Bhagavad gītā*, 3 vols. (Madras: Educational Pub. Co. [1957–66]).

Ranganathananda, Swami, *Universal Message of the Bhagavad Gītā: An Exposition of the Gītā in the Light of Modern*

Thought and Modern Needs (Calcutta: Advaita Ashrama, 2000).

Ravi, Illa, *Foundations of Indian Ethics: With Special Reference to Manu smṛti, Jaimini sūtras, and Bhagavad-Gītā* (New Delhi: Kaveri Books, 2002).

Resnick, Howard J., 'Kṛṣṇa in the Bhagavad Gītā: A Beginning Ontology from the Gaudiya Perspective', *Journal of Vaiṣṇava Studies*, 3 (Spring 1995), 5–32.

Rocher, Ludo, '*Bhagavadgita* 2.20 and *Kathopanishad* 2.18: A New Interpretation', *Adyar Library Bulletin*, 27 (1963), 45–58.

Rosen, Steven, *Holy War: Violence and the Bhagavadgita* (Hampton, Va.: Deepak Heritage Books, 2002).

——, *Gita on the Green: The Mystical Tradition Behind Bagger Vance* (New York: Continuum, 2000).

Roy, S. C., *The Bhagavad Gita and Modern Scholarship* (London: Luzac and Co., 1941).

Schreiner, Peter, *Bhagavad-Gītā: Wege und Weisungen* (Zurich: Benziger, 1991).

Selvanayagam, I., 'Pointers and Particulars for an Historical Approach to Hindu Religious Texts: The Case of the Bhagavad Gita', in David C. Scott and I. Selvanayagam (eds.), *Re-visioning India's Religious Traditions: Essays in Honour of Eric Lott* (Delhi: ISPCK, 1996), 22–46.

——, 'Ashoka and Arjuna as Counterfigures Standing on the Field of Dharma', *History of Religions*, 32/1 (1992), 57–75.

Sharma, Arvind, 'The Bhagavadgita: A Mimamsic Approach', in Braj M. Sinha (ed.), *The Contemporary Essays on the Bhagavad Gita* (New Delhi: Siddharth Publications, 1995).

——, 'Some Early Anticipations of the Gandhian Intepretation of the Bhagavad-Gītā', in Victor C. Hayes (ed.), *Australian Essays in World Religion* (Bedford Park: Australian Assoc. for the Study of Religions, 1977), 66–72.

Sharpe, Eric J., *The Universal Gītā: Western Images of the Bhagavad Gītā. A Bicentenary Survey* (LaSalle, Ill.: Open Court, 1985).

——, 'Some Western Interpretations of the Bhagavad Gītā,

1785–1885', in Peter Slater and Donald Weibe (eds.), *Traditions in Contact and Change* (Waterloo, Canada: Wilfried Laurier University Press, 1983), 65–85.

——, 'Protestant Missionaries and the Study of the Bhagavad Gītā', *International Bulletin of Missionary Research*, 6 (Oct. 1982), 155–9.

Shideler, Emerson W., 'Meaning of Man in the Bhagavad Gita', *Journal of Bible and Religion*, 28/3 (July 1960), 308–16.

Sinha, Braj M. (ed.), *The Contemporary Essays on the Bhagavad Gita* (New Delhi: Siddharth Publications, 1995).

Sircar, Mahendranath, *Mysticism in the Bhagavad-gītā* (Calcutta: S. C. Seal, Bhāratī Mahāvidyālaya, 1944).

Smith, R. Morton, 'Statistics of the Bhagavadgītā', *Journal of the Ganganatha Jha Research Institute*, 24/104 (1968), 39–46.

Thomas, P. M., *20th Century Indian Interpretations of Bhagavadgītā: Tilak, Gandhi and Aurobindo* (Delhi: ISPCK, 1987).

Tilak, G. B., *Gītārahasya*, trans. Balchandra Sitaram Sukthankar (Poona: Tilak Bros, 1971 [1893]).

Tucker, Janet, *The Bhagavad Gītā: An Aid to Study* (Roehampton: Roehampton Religious Studies Monographs, 1983).

Upadhyaya, K. N., *Early Buddhism and the Bhagavad Gita* (Delhi: Motilal Banarsidass, 1971).

Van Buitenen, J. A. B., 'A Contribution to the Critical Edition of the *Bhagavadgītā*', *Journal of the American Oriental Society*, 85 (Jan.–March 1965), 99–109.

Venkateswaran, R. J., *Bhagavad Gita for Peace of Mind* (Bombay: Bharatiya Vidya Bhavan, 1982).

von Humboldt, William, 'Über die unter dem Namen Bhagavadgītā bekannte Episode des Mahābhārata', *K. Academie der Wissenschaften zu Berlin, Philosophische-historische Klasse, Abhandlungen* (1826), 1–64.

Woodhead, Linda, 'Simone Weil's Conversation with the Bhagavad Gita', *Theology*, 90 (Jan. 1987), 24–32.

——, '"Standing on the Peak": A Concept Common to the Bhagavad-Gita and the Victorines', in Alexander Altmann *et al.* (eds.), *Studies in Mysticism and Religion Presented to Gershom G. Scholem on his 70th Birthday* (Jerusalem: Magnes Press, Hebrew University, 1967), 381–7.

SELECT SANSKRIT COMMENTARIES

Adidevana, Swami, *Shri Ramanuja Gita Bhashya*, trans. and ed. Svami Adidevananda (Madras: Sri Ramakrishna Math, 1991).

Belvalkar, S. K., *Śrīmadbhagavadgītā (with Commentary of Anandavardhana)* (Punyapattane: Bilvakunja Prakashana Samsthan, 1941).

Marjanovic, Boris (ed. and trans.), *Gitārtha Saṃgraha: Abhinavagupta's Commentary on the Bhagavad Gītā* (Varanasi: Indica Books, 2002).

Sadhale, Gajanana Sambhu (ed.), *Śrīmadbhagavadgītā: Śaṅkarabhāṣyodyekādaśasaṭīkopetā/ with Eleven Commentaries*, 3 vols., Parimal Sanskrit series, 17 (Delhi: Parimala Pablikesansa, 1985).

Śaṅkarācārya, *Śrīmad Bhagavad Gītā bhāṣya* of Śrī Śaṁkarācarya, trans. A. G. Krishna Warrier (Madras: Sri Ramakrishna Math, 1983).

——, *The Bhagavad Gītā: With the Commentary of Śrī Śaṅkarācharya*, trans. Alladi Mahadeva Sastry (Madras: Samata Books, 1979 [1977]).

Śāstrī, Jīvarāma Lallurama (ed.), *Śrīmadbhagavadgītā: Tattvaprakāśiketyadyāṣṭaṭīkopetā/saṃsodhanakartā, with Eight Commentaries*, 3 vols., ed. Jivarama Lallurama Sastri, Mahadevasarma Bakre and Dinakara Visnu Gokhale, Parimal Sanskrit series, 59 (Delhi: Parimala Pablikesansa, 2001 [Bombay: Gujarati Printing Press, 1915]).

Van Buitenen, J. A. B., *Rāmānuja on the Bhagavadgītā* (New Delhi: Motilal Banarsidass, 1968).

OTHER ENGLISH TRANSLATIONS

Arnold, Edwin (trans.), *Bhagavad Gita; the Song Celestial: The Sanskrit-text, Translated into English Verse*, with an introduction by Sri Prakasa, illustrated with paintings by Y. G. Srimati (New York: Heritage Press, 1965 [1885]).

Besant, Annie (trans.), *The Bhagavad Gītā; or, The Lord's Song*, 3rd Adyar edn. (Madras: Theosophical Publishing House, 1953).

Chatterji, Mohini M. (trans.), *The Bhagavad Gītā: or The Lord's Lay*, preface by Ainslie Embree (New York: Julian Press, 1960).

De Nicolás, Antonio T. (trans.), *The Bhagavad Gita: The Ethics of Decision-making* (Berwick, Me.: Nicolas-Hays, 2004).

Deutsch, Eliot (trans.), *The Bhagavad Gītā* (New York: Holt, Rinehart, and Winston, 1968).

Easwaran, Eknath (trans.), *The Bhagavad Gita* (New York: Vintage Books, 2000).

Edgerton, Franklin (trans.), *The Bhagavad gītā*, 2 vols. (Cambridge, Mass.: Harvard University Press; London: H. Milford, Oxford University Press, 1944).

Feuerstein, Georg (trans.), *The Bhagavad-Gītā: Yoga of Contemplation and Action* (New Delhi: Arnold-Heinemann, 1981; Atlantic Highlands, NJ: Humanities Press, 1981).

Gotshalk, Richard (trans.), *Bhagavad Gītā* (Delhi: Motilal Banarsidass, 1985).

Herman, A. L. (trans.), *The Bhagavad Gītā: A Translation and Critical Commentary* (Springfield, Ill.: C. C. Thomas, 1973).

Johnson, W. J. (trans.), *Bhagavad Gita* (Oxford and New York: Oxford University Press, 1994).

Johnston, Charles (trans.), *Bhagavad Gita: The Song of the Master* (London: J. M. Watkins, 1965 [1908]).

Kaushika, Asoka (ed.), *Srīmad Bhagavadgītā/sampādaka*, Romanisation and English trans. Janak Datt (New Delhi: Star Publications, 2000).

Lal, P. (trans.), *The Bhagavad Gita* (Calcutta: Writers Workshop, 1974).

Mahesh Yogi, Maharishi (trans.), *Maharishi Mahesh Yogi on the Bhagavad-gita: A New Translation and Commentary with Sanskrit text. Chapters 1 to 6* (Harmondsworth: Penguin, 1969).

Mascaró, Juan (trans.), *The Bhagavad Gita* (Baltimore: Penguin Books, 1962).

Miller, Barbara Stoler (trans.), *The Bhagavad-Gita: Krishna's Counsel in Time of War*, with an introduction and afterword by Barbara Stoler Miller (New York: Bantam Books, 1986).

Mitchell, Stephen (trans.), *Bhagavad Gita: A New Translation* (New York: Harmony Books, 2000).

Murthy, Srinivasa (trans.), *The Bhagavad Gītā*, with introduction and notes by B. Srinivasa Murthy (Long Beach, Calif.: Long Beach Publications, 1985).

Nataraja Guru (trans.), *The Bhagavad Gītā; A Sublime Hymn of Dialectics Composed by the Antique Sage-bard Vyāsa* (Bombay and New York: Asia Pub. House, 1962).

Nikhilananda, Swami (trans.), *The Bhagavad Gītā*, with notes, comments and introduction by Swami Nikhilananda (New York: Ramakrishna-Vivekananda Center, 1944).

Parrinder, Geoffrey, *The Bhagavad Gītā: A Verse Translation* (New Delhi: Research Press, 1999).

Prabhavananda, Swami, and Isherwood, Christopher (trans.), *Bhagavad-Gita, The Song of God*, introduction by Aldous Huxley (New York: New American Library, 1951).

Prabhupāda, A. C. Bhaktivedanta Swami (trans.), *Bhagavad-gītā as It Is*, complete edn., revised and enlarged (New York: Bhaktivedanta Book Trust, 1991 [1986]).

Sargeant, Winthrop (trans.), *The Bhagavad Gītā*, rev. edn. (Albany, NY: State University of New York Press, 1984).

Sarma, D. S. (trans.), *The Bhagavad Gita, Students' Edition* (Madras: Current Thought Press, 1930).

Senart, Émile (trans.), *La Bhagavad-gîtâ*, with an introduction by Émile Senart, 2nd edn. with facing text (Paris: Les Belles Lettres, 1922).

Stanford, Ann (trans.), *The Bhagavad Gita: A New Verse Translation* (New York: Herder and Herder, 1970).

Van Buitenen, J. A. B. (trans.), *The Bhagavad Gītā in the*

Mahābhārata: A Bilingual Edition (Chicago: University of Chicago Press, 1981).

Vaswani, T. L. (trans.), *The Bhagavad Gītā: The Song of Life*, ed. J. P. Vaswani (Poona: Gita Pub. House, n.d.).

Vireswaranda, Swami (trans.), *Śrīmad-Bhagavad-Gītā: Text, Translation of the Text and of the Gloss of Śrīdhara Swami* (Mylapore: Sri Ramakrishna Math, 1948).

White, David (trans.), *The Bhagavad Gītā: A New Translation with Commentary* (New York: P. Lang, 1988).

Wood, Ernest (trans.), *The Bhagavad Gita Explained* (Los Angeles: New Century Book Shop, 1954).

Zaehner, R. C. (trans.), *The Bhagavad-Gītā, with a Commentary Based on the Original Sources* (Oxford: Clarendon Press, 1969).

The *Gita* has been translated into a myriad of Indian languages as well as European ones (over 1,800 translations in more than 75 languages). In India and other parts of South Asia, I have been able to locate translations into and commentaries in Assamese, Avadhi, Benali, Bhojpuri, Braj, Dogri, Gujarati, Hindi, Ho Mundari, Kanauji, Kannada, Kashmiri, Khasi, Konkani, Kuamoni, Maithili, Malayalam, Malvi, Manipuri, Marathi, Marvari, Mevari, Nepali, Oriya, Prakrit, Punjabi, Santali, Sindhi, Sinhala, Tamil, Teluga, Tibetan and Urdu.

In European languages, I have found translations into Czech, Danish, Dutch, Finnish, French, French Creole, Georgian, German, Modern Greek, Hungarian, Icelandic, Italian, Latin, Lithuanian, Norwegian, Polish, Portuguese, Romanian, Russian, Serbo-Croat, Slovak, Solvenian, Spanish, Swedish and Yiddish.

In Asian and Semitic languages, there are Arabic, Bahasa, Balinese, Chinese, Hebrew, Japanese, Old Javanese, Malagasy, Mongolian, Persian and Thai translations.

THE BHAGAVAD GITA

THE FIRST DISCOURSE

Dhritarashtra said:

1
Sanjaya,
when my sons
and the sons of Pandu
had gathered,
longing to fight
in the field of *dharma*,
the field of Kuru,
what did they do?

Sanjaya said:

2
When he truly saw
the force
of the Pandavas
gathered together,
Duryodhana
approached
Drona the teacher,
and said these words:[1]

3
'Master,
look at the sons
of Pandu –

the great army
drawn up
by Drupada's son –[2]
one of your own
wise students.

4

Great heroes
who throw the arrow
in the same way
as Bhima and Arjuna
in battle:
Yuyudhana and Virata,
and Drupada,
with the great chariot.[3]

5

Dhrishtasaketu,
the bold leader,
and Cekitana,
the intelligent one;
and the brave King of Kashi;
Purujit, who conquers widely,
and Kuntibhoja,[4]
and Shaibya, both bull and man.

6

Mighty Yudhamanyu,
passionate in battle,
and Uttamaujas
most powerful;
the son of Subhadra,
and the sons of Draupadi,
all indeed
with great chariots.[5]

7

And, on our side too,
there are those
who are distinguished;
recognize them,
highest of the twice-born.
I will name them for you
so that you will know
these leaders of my army.

8

You, Drona,
and Bhishma,
and Karna,
and Kripa,
always victorious
in battle,
and the son
of Somadatta too.[6]

9

And many others –
heroes who
are ready
to give up life
for my sake –
throwing many
different weapons,
all skilled in battle.

10

This force
of ours
guarded by Bhishma
is unbounded;
although this force,

of theirs –
guarded by Bhima,
is bounded.[7]

11

All of you,
truly honourable ones,
must indeed
protect Bhishma[8]
in all manoeuvres,
each holding down
his own place,
as appropriate.'

12

Giving Duryodhana
great joy,
Bhishma,
the old Kuru grandfather,
crying a high
lion's roar,
with full force
blew his conch horn;

13

then the conch horns
and kettledrums,
the cymbals, drums,
bull-mouth trumpets,
all suddenly
were sounded,
and the sound grew
into great tumult.

14

Then, standing
with white horses
yoked in a great,

swift chariot,
Krishna, son of Madhu,
and Arjuna, son of Pandu,
both blew
their divine conch horns.

15
The bristling-haired Krishna[9]
blew the horn
called Pancajanya;
Arjuna, winner of wealth,
blew the horn Devadatta;
and wolf-bellied Bhima,
awesome in his deeds,
blew the horn Paundra.

16
Kunti's son, King Yudhishthira,
blew the horn Endless Victory,
called Anantavijaya;
Nakula and Sahadeva
both blew the two horns
Lovely Sound, called Sughosha,
and Chalice of Gems,
called Manipushpaka.

17
The One from Kashi,
the highest bowman,
and Shikhandin
with the great chariot,
Dhrishthadyumna,
and Virata,
and Satyaki,
still unconquered;[10]

18
Ruler of the Earth:
Drupada of swift step,
and the Sons of Draupadi,
all together,
and the strong-armed
Son of Subhadra,
they blew conch horns
one by one.

19
The great cry
tore the hearts
of the Sons
of Dhritarashtra;
the tumult
made the sky
and the earth
resound.

20
When he saw
the sons of Dhritarashtra
drawn up in battle array
in the emerging
clash of weapons,
the Son of Pandu,
with his monkey banner,
raised his bow.[11]

21
Then straight-haired Arjuna
spoke these words
to bristling-haired Krishna:
'Lord of the Earth,
Unchanging One,

make my chariot stand
in the middle of
the two armies,

22
until I see fully
these men drawn up
in a hunger
for battle.
With whom
must I fight
in beginning
this battle?

23
I see those
who are about to fight –
those who have
gathered here,
wishing to do
loving service in battle
for the hard-souled son
of Dhritarashtra.'

24
Son of Bharata:
in this way,
bristling-haired Krishna
was spoken to
by thick-haired Arjuna,[12]
while Krishna made
the great chariot
stand between both armies.

25
Facing Bhishma
and Drona
and all the rulers

of the world,
Arjuna,
son of Pritha, said,
'Look at the Kurus,
gathered in this way!'

26

Arjuna, son of Pritha,
saw fathers,
and then grandfathers
standing there –
teachers, mother's brothers,
brothers, sons,
grandsons,
and friends, too;

27

fathers-in-law,
and companions
of strong heart.
Looking at all
his relatives
come together
in both armies,
the son of Kunti[13]

28

broke down
with deep compassion
and said,
'Krishna, now that
I have seen
my own people here,
coming near and
longing to fight,

29
my legs
collapse,
my mouth
is parched,
my body
trembles,
and my hair
bristles;[14]

30
the Gandiva bow
drops from my hand,
my skin
is burned,
and I find
no rest;
my mind
seems to wander;

31
I see
perverse omens;
and before me
I see no good
in killing
my people
in battle,
Lovely-Haired Krishna!

32
Krishna, I long
neither for victory,
nor kingship
nor pleasures.
Lord of the Cows,[15]

what is kingship to us,
what are delights,
or life itself?

33

The ones
on whose behalf
we long for kingship,
delights, and pleasures –
these are the very ones
drawn up in battle,
giving up
life-breath and wealth![16]

34

Teachers,
fathers and sons
and grandfathers, too,
mother's brothers,
fathers-in-law
grandsons,
brothers-in-law –
also other family –

35

Killer of Madhu,[17]
even though they
are ready to kill,
I don't want to kill them –
even for the kingship
of the three worlds,
and certainly not
for the earth.

36

Mover of Men,
what joy would it be
for us to kill

the sons of Dhritarashtra?
Evil would still cling to us
when we'd killed
these men here,
with their bows drawn.

37
Therefore we are not
entitled to kill
the sons of Dhritarashtra,
our own kinsmen.
After we had killed
our own people,
how would we take pleasure,
Son of Madhu?[18]

38
Even if those whose thoughts
are overwhelmed by greed
do not see the wrong done
by the destruction
of family,
and the fault
of meanness
and injury to friends,

39
Mover of Men,
how would we not know
through clear vision
to turn away
from this evil –
the wrong done
by the destruction
of family?

40

In the destruction
of family,
the eternal *dharma*
of family perishes;
when *dharma* perishes,
its absence
also conquers
the whole family.

41

Son of Vrishni,[19]
when the absence
of *dharma* has conquered,
the women of the family
are defiled,
and caste-confusion is born
in the corruption
of women;[20]

42

the caste-blending
of the family
and the family-destroyers
indeed brings them hell:
bereft of offerings
of rice and water,[21]
their ancestors
will surely fall.

43

The *dharma* of caste,
and the eternal *dharma*
of family,
are uprooted
by these wrongful acts
of family-destroyers,
since they create
a blending of caste.[22]

44
Mover of Men,
those humans
whose *dharma*
has vanished
will live
for ever in hell;
we have heard this
over and over again.

45
Oh! we are set
upon doing
a great harm;
we are eager to kill
our own people,
all for the sake
of pleasure
and a kingdom.

46
If the sons
of Dhritarashtra,
weapons in hand,
should strike me
unarmed in battle,
this would be
greater peace
for me!'

47
After he spoke,
Arjuna sat down
on the chariot seat,
in the midst of battle,
and let go of
both his bow and arrow,
his whole being
recoiling in grief.

THE SECOND DISCOURSE

Sanjaya said:

1

Krishna,
Killer of Madhu,
spoke these words
to the despairing one
whose eyes were
filled with tears,
and who was overcome
with pity.

The Blessed One said:

2

How does
this faint heart
come to you
in time of difficulty?
This is not suitable
for a noble one;[1]
it is not heavenly,
and brings on disgrace.

3

Do not become
a cowardly eunuch,[2]
Son of Pritha;

this is not fitting for you.
Let go of this
lowly weakness of the heart
and stand up,
Scorcher of the Enemy![3]

Arjuna said:

4
Killer of Madhu,
how will I fight
Drona and Bhishma
with arrows
in battle?
How will I fight
these honourable men,
Killer of the Enemy?

5
Better to eat beggar's food
than to kill these great-souled
teachers here on earth;
for if I killed these teachers,
striving after their goals
here on earth,
I would eat food
covered in blood.

6
Facing the sons
of Dhritarashtra,
we do not know
which has more weight for us:
should we conquer them,
or should they conquer us?
Even after we've killed them,
we would not want to live!

7

My own nature is struck
by pity, and a sense of wrong,
and my mind is clouded
as to *dharma*:
I ask you which is best –
tell me! I am your student!
Correct me, who lies
fallen before your feet.

8

I don't ever see
what would take away
my grief – that grief
which dries up the senses,
even though I might gain
opulent and unrivalled
kingship here on earth,
or even lordship of the gods.[4]

Sanjaya said:

9

Scorcher of the Enemy,[5]
after speaking
to bristling-haired Krishna,
thick-haired Arjuna
said: 'I will not fight!'
He spoke this way
to Krishna, the cow finder,
and then became quiet.

10

Son of Bharata,
bristling-haired Krishna
seemed to
begin to laugh,
and in between

both armies,
spoke these words
to the despairing one:

The Blessed One said:

11

You speak as if
with words of wisdom,
[but] you have mourned
that which is
not to be mourned.
Wise men mourn neither
those whose life-breath is gone,
nor those whose breath remains.

12

I have never
not existed;
nor have you, nor have
these lords of men.
Nor will we
cease to exist,
all of us,
from now onwards.

13

Just as childhood,
youth and age
exist in the body
of the embodied self,[6]
in this way, one takes on
another body.
Those who see clearly
are not confused by this.

14
Son of Kunti,
the touches of the senses,
bringing pain and pleasure,
heat and cold:
they come and go,
and they don't last for ever.
You must try to endure them,
son of Bharata.[7]

15
Bull among Men,
the one whom
these touches
do not make tremble,
the one for whom
pain and pleasure are alike,
that one is ready
for immortality.

16
Being is not found
in that which does not exist.
Non-being is not found
in that which exists.
The limit of both
being and non-being
is perceived by those
who see the truth.

17
Know this:
that with which
all this world is woven
is not to be destroyed.
No one is able

to effect
the destruction
of the imperishable.

18

These bodies
have an end;
but they are said
to belong to the eternal
embodied self –
that which is never lost
and cannot be measured.
So fight, Son of Bharata!

19

The one who perceives
the self as a killer,
and the one who perceives
the self as killed:
neither of them know
that this self
does not kill,
nor is it killed.

20

The self is not born
nor does it ever die.
Once it has been, this self will
never cease to be again.
Unborn,[8] eternal,
continuing from the old,
the self is not killed
when the body is killed.[9]

21

The one who
knows the eternal
and the indestructible,

that which is unborn,
and imperishable,
how does he cause to die,
Son of Pritha, and whom?
How does he kill, and whom?

22

Just as one
throws out old clothes
and then takes on
other, new ones;
so the embodied self
casts out old bodies
as it gets
other, new ones.

23

Weapons do not
cut the self,
nor does fire
burn it,
nor do waters
drench it,
nor does wind
dry it.

24

The self
is not to be pierced,
nor burned,
nor drenched,
nor dried;
it is eternal,
all-pervading and fixed –
unmoving from the beginning.

25

The self
is not readily seen;
by sight or mind;
it is said to be formless
and unchanging;
so, when you
have known this,
you should not mourn.

26

And even
if you think
the self *is*
eternally born,
or eternally dead –
still, you should not
mourn it,
Strong-Armed One.[10]

27

Death is fixed
for those
who are born,
and birth is fixed
for those who die;
since such an end
is certain,
you should not grieve.

28

Son of Bharata,
beings have beginnings
which are formless,
and middle states
which do have form,

and deaths which,
again, are formless;
why would one grieve over this?

29
It is a wonder
that anyone sees this,
and a wonder
that anyone else speaks it,
and a wonder
that yet another hears it.
Yet even when they've heard it,
no one knows it at all.

30
Son of Bharata,
the embodied self
which exists in the body
of everyone
is eternally
free from harm;
so you should not grieve
for any living beings.

31
And as you discern
your own *dharma*,
you should not waver.
For the warrior,
there can be found
nothing greater
than battle
for the sake of *dharma*.

32
And if the open door
of heaven
is reached

by happy accident,
then warriors take pleasure
when they find
such a battle,
Son of Pritha.

33

If you will not
engage this fight
for the sake
of *dharma*,
you will have shunned
your own *dharma*
and good name,
and shall cause harm.

34

And people
will tell stories
of your own
eternal disgrace;
and for those
who are esteemed,
disgrace
surpasses death.

35

The warriors
in their great chariots
will think you shrank
from the joys of battle
because of fear;
and where they once
thought of you highly,
they will now think you unworthy.

36

And those who are
hostile to you
will speak
many unspeakable words,
ridiculing
your power.
What greater pain
is there?

37

If you are killed,
you shall reach heaven;
or if you triumph,
you shall enjoy the earth;
so stand up,
Son of Kunti,
firm in your resolve
to fight!

38

When you have made
pleasure and pain the same –
also gain and loss,
and victory and defeat,
then join yourself
to battle;
and in this way,
you will not cause harm.

39

Son of Pritha,
this insight has been spoken
to you in terms of *samkhya*;
now hear it
in terms of *yoga*;

joined to this insight,
you will avoid
the bonds of action.[11]

40

In this *yoga*,
no effort
goes to waste,
and no momentum
is lost;
even a little
of this *dharma*
rescues one from great fear.

41

Joy of the Kurus,
this insight here
is firm in nature,
and singular,
but the insights
of those who waver
are endless,
with many branches.

42

The ones who
do not see
proclaim
this overblown speech;
passionate
in the world of Veda[12]
they declare,
'There is nothing else!'

43

Their nature is desire,
with heaven as their object;
they turn to

different rituals
whose aim is power
and consumption,
but whose fruit of action
is really rebirth.

44

To those clinging
to consumption
and power,
whose thoughts are stolen by this,
that insight
whose nature is firm
is not given
in meditation.

45

Arjuna, the Vedas
belong to the three *guna*s,
and you must be free
of the three *guna*s,
free from opposites,[13]
eternally dwelling in truth,
neither acquiring nor keeping,
self-possessed.

46

For a brahmin
who discerns,
there is as much value
in all the Vedas
as there is
in a well
when water overflows
on every side.

47

Your authority is
in action alone,
and never
in its fruits;
motive should never be
in the fruits of action,
nor should you cling
to inaction.[14]

48

Abiding in *yoga*,
engage in actions!
Let go of clinging,
and let fulfilment
and frustration
be the same;
for it is said
yoga is equanimity.

49

Winner of Wealth,
action is far inferior
to the *yoga* of insight.
Look for refuge
in insight;
for those who are
motivated by fruits
are to be pitied.

50

The one who is
joined to insight
casts off
both good
and evil acts.
So join yourself
to *yoga*;
yoga is ease in action.

51
The wise ones
joined to insight,
and who have
let go of the fruit,
freed from
the bonds of birth,
they go to that place
which is without pain.

52
When your insight
crosses well beyond
the tangle of confusion,
then you will
become disillusioned
with those revelations
which had been heard,
and may be heard [again].[15]

53
When your insight
is in deep focus,
and when it stands
motionless,
ignoring the revelation
which had been heard,
then you will
reach *yoga*.

Arjuna said:

54
Lovely-Haired One,
what language is there
for a person
whose wisdom is firm
and meditation steady?

How would the one
whose thoughts are firm
speak? Or sit? Or move about?

The Blessed One said:

55
Son of Pritha,
when a person renounces
all the desires
in the mind,
that one is said
to be content
in the self, by the self,
and firm in wisdom.

56
The person whose mind
is free from anxiety
about sorrows,
and free from greed
for pleasures,
with rage, passion and fear gone,
whose thoughts are firm,
that one is said to be a sage.

57
The person who has
no longing anywhere,
coming across
this and that,
pure and impure,
who neither loves nor hates,
that one's wisdom
stands firm.

58
When a person
draws in the senses
from the sense-objects
in every sphere,
like a tortoise
pulls in its limbs,
that one's wisdom
stands firm.

59
These spheres of sense
fall away from the
embodied self
who continues to fast –
all except taste;
and then taste, too,
falls away from the one
who has seen the highest.[16]

60
Son of Kunti,
the senses tear apart
and violently seize
the mind –
even for one
who makes great effort,
and who knows
the tremor of reality.[17]

61
The person who
has practised *yoga*,
restraining all these senses,
should sit,
with me as a pinnacle;

the one whose senses
are in control –
that one's wisdom stands firm.

62

Clinging is born
to someone
who dwells on
the spheres of the senses;
desire is born
from clinging;
and anger is born
from desire.

63

Confusion arises
from anger;
and from confusion
memory strays;
from the fall of memory
comes the loss of insight;
and one is lost
when one's insight is lost.

64

One not joined
to passion and hatred,
always moving
in the spheres of the senses
by the senses,
the one who thus restrains the self,
and who governs the self,
attains peace.

65

In calmness,
there occurs
the withdrawal

of all pain;
for that person
whose thought is placid,
insight becomes steady
right away.

66

There is no insight
for one who has not
practised *yoga*;
there is no peace
for the one
who does not concentrate;[18]
and from where does pleasure come
for the one who has no peace?

67

When the mind
is led by
the roving senses,
then it steals
one's wisdom,
like the wind
steals a ship
on the water.

68

Strong-Armed One,
the wisdom
of the person
who has drawn in
the senses
from their objects
in every sphere,
that one's wisdom stands firm.

69

The restrained one
is watchful
during the night
of all beings;
and in the time
when beings are watchful,
that is the night
of the sage who sees.[19]

70

As the ocean becomes full,
yet is steady and unmoved
as the waters enter it,
so the one whom
all desires enter
in this way gains peace;
yet this is not so for
the one who desires desire.[20]

71

The person who
casts away all desires,
who moves away from clinging,
who has no idea
of 'mine',
and who has no idea
of 'I',
that one comes to peace.[21]

72

Son of Pritha,
this is the state of Brahman;
if one has not reached this,
one is confused.
But firm in this,
even at the time of ending,
one reaches Brahman,
the bliss of cessation.[22]

THE THIRD DISCOURSE

Arjuna said:

1

Mover of Men,
if your idea is
that insight is stronger
than action,
then why do you
enjoin me
to such terrible action,[1]
Lovely-Haired One?

2

Through words
that seem contradictory,
you confuse
my insight;
tell me one thing
that is without doubt –
how might I reach
the higher good?

The Blessed One said:

3

Blameless One,
in this world,
a double foundation

was taught by me in ancient times:
the *yoga* of knowledge
for those who follow *samkhya*,
and the *yoga* of action
for those who practise *yoga*.[2]

4

One does not reach
the state
beyond action[3]
by abstaining
from actions;
nor does one
reach fulfilment
only by renunciation.

5

No one, not even
for one moment,
ever stands without acting;
by virtue of the *guna*s
born in nature,
without willing it,
everyone is made
to perform action.

6

The person who sits
and subdues
the active senses,
while remembering and mindful
of the objects of the senses:
it is said that such a one
is a confused self –
who proceeds falsely.

7

But, Arjuna,
the one who begins
to rein in the senses
through the mind
and who, without clinging,
begins the *yoga* of action
through the active senses,
is unique.

8

So perform action
which is restrained,
for this action is better
than non-action;
and even the working
of your body
would not succeed
without action.

9

Except for action
whose end is sacrifice,
this world is bound by action;
without clinging,
perform action
towards this end
of sacrifice,
Son of Kunti.

10

In ancient times,
after he created
sacrifices
along with humans,
the lord of beings said:

'You shall create through this!
May this be the cow
who grants your desires.

11

By this, may you
cause the gods to be;
and may the gods
cause you to be.
As you both
sustain each other,
you will reach
the higher good.'[4]

12

As the gods are created
by sacrifice,
they will give you
sought-after pleasures.
The one who enjoys
what is given by them
but does not give to them
is a thief.

13

The true ones who eat
the leftovers
of the sacrifices
are free from all evils;
but the evil ones
eat their own impurity,
as they cook
only for themselves.[5]

14

Beings exist
through food;
Parjanya, the rain,

is the source of food.
Parjanya exists
through sacrifice
and sacrifice
exists through action.[6]

15
Know the origin
of sacrificial action
as Brahman, arising from
the eternal nature[7]
of Brahman;
thus all-pervading Brahman
is eternally fixed
in sacrifice.

16
The one who does not
set the wheel
in motion
here on earth
lives uselessly,
wanting to hurt,
impassioned by the senses,
Son of Pritha.

17
The person
who would be content
in the self,
pleased in the self,
happy in the self –
for that one,
a reason for action
does not exist.

18

For that person,
there is no goal in action,
nor any goal
in non-action;
and that one
does not cling to goals,
in connection with
any beings.

19

So, without clinging,
always perform
actions to be done.
When one performs
actions to be done
without clinging,
one attains
the highest.

20

By action alone,
King Janaka
and many others
gained fulfilment.[8]
Observing even
the simple maintenance
of the world,
you should act!

21

As the best person
practises
in various pursuits,
so too will the rest.
That one sets

the standard
that the world
then follows.

22
Son of Pritha:
for me, nothing at all
is to be done
in the three worlds;
there is nothing
to be reached
which has not been reached.
Even so, I move in action.

23
Surely if I,
who am inexhaustible,
did not undertake
any action at all,
humankind would
follow my path
everywhere,
Son of Pritha.

24
If I did not
perform actions,
these worlds
would sink down;
I would be a creator
of scattered confusion,
and I would destroy
these human beings.

25
Son of Bharata,
just as the unwise ones act
while clinging to action,

so the wise should act
without clinging,
but rather, wanting
to keep the world
collected together.[9]

26

One should not give birth
to the shredding of insight
among the ignorant
who cling to action:
the wise one, acting
while joined to *yoga*,
should cause them
to delight in all action.

27

Everywhere
actions are performed
by the *guna*s
of nature.
The Self, confused
by the idea of an 'I',
thus thinks,
'I am the doer.'

28

Strong-Armed One,
when the person who knows
the truth of the two spheres –
of *guna* and action –
thinks, 'The *guna*s
are merely revolving
among the *guna*s,'
then that person does not cling.

29

Those who are confused
by the *guna*s of nature
cling to the actions
of those *guna*s.
The one who knows the whole
should not disturb
the fools who
do not know the whole.

30

When you have entrusted
all actions to me,
with thought
on the highest self,
when you have become
free from desire,
free from the idea of 'mine',
then fight, with grief gone.

31

Those who
eternally follow
this thought
of mine,
full of trust,
who do not sneer –
they are freed,
even by actions.

32

But recognize
that those who sneer,
and who do not follow
this idea
of mine,

are lost
and thoughtless,
confusing all wisdom.

33
Even the wise person
struggles
according to
individual nature;
beings follow
their own nature.
So what will
restraint accomplish?

34
Passion and hatred
abide in the place
between a sense
and its object;
one should not
come under the will
of these two –
one's enemies on the path.

35
Better one's own *dharma*,
even if ineffective,
than the *dharma*
of another, practised well!
Better death
in one's own *dharma*!
The *dharma* of another
only brings on fear.

Arjuna said:

36
Son of Vrishni,
then what
sets a person
in motion
to do harm,
even unintentionally,
as if driven
by force?

The Blessed One said:

37
Learn the enemy,
here on earth:
it is desire and anger;
the *guna of rajas*,
or passion,
is their source.
Each is all-consuming
and evil.

38
As fire, bearer of oblations,
is covered by smoke,
and as a mirror
is covered by dust,
and as an embryo
is covered by the womb,
so this wisdom
is covered by this.

39
Son of Kunti,
the wisdom of the wise
is covered by

this eternal enemy;
covered by a fire
in the shape of desire,
a fire which is
always hungry.[10]

40

It is said
that the dwelling place of desire
is insight, mind
and the senses.
Through these,
desire covers wisdom
and confuses
the embodied self.

41

So, Bull of the Bharatas:
first rein in
the senses;
then strike down
this evil one
who destroys
wisdom
and discernment.

42

They say
that the senses are crucial;
and the mind more crucial
than the senses;
and even more crucial
than the mind is insight;
and much more crucial
than insight, is this [self].

43
Strong-Armed One,
when you have learned
what is higher than insight –
the self, sustained
through the self –
then kill the enemy
that takes the shape of desire
and is hard to approach.

THE FOURTH DISCOURSE

The Blessed One said:

1

I declared
this imperishable *yoga*
to Vivasvat,
god of the sun,
and he told it to Manu,
the first human,
who told it
to his son Ikshvaku.

2

Scorcher of the Enemy,
through many an age,
the royal sages
knew this *yoga*,
obtained as it was
through lineage;
and then this *yoga*
was lost to the world.

3

Today I tell
this ancient *yoga* to you,
since you
are devoted to me,
and since you

are my friend.
This is indeed
the highest mystery.

Arjuna said:

4

But your birth
was later,
and the birth of Vivasvat
was earlier;
how should I
understand
that you spoke it
in the beginning?

The Blessed One said:

5

Arjuna,
many of my births
have come and gone,
and yours, too;
while I know
them all,
you do not,
Scorcher of the Enemy.

6

Although I am unborn,
an imperishable self,
and the Lord
of all Beings,
I govern my own
earthly nature,
and come into being
by my own creative force.

7

Son of Bharata,
whenever there is
a decline
in *dharma*,
and the absence
of *dharma*
increases,
I create myself.[1]

8

I come into being
from age to age
with the purpose
of fixing *dharma* –
as a refuge for
those who do good
and as a doom
for those who do evil.

9

So Arjuna,
when one who truly knows
my divine
birth and action
leaves the body,
that person does not
go to birth again,
but goes to me.

10

Thinking of me,
resorting to me,
many have reached
my being, purified
through the heated discipline

of wisdom,
their greed, fear and anger
fully gone.

11

Son of Pritha,
I devote myself
to those
who resort to me;
in just the same way,
people follow
my path
in all places.

12

Longing for fulfilment
through ritual acts,
here in this world,
they sacrifice to the gods;
and in this mortal world,
fulfilment born of such acts
comes into being
quickly indeed.

13

The four castes were brought forth
by me, distributing
*guna*s with actions;
although I am
the Creator of this world,
know me
as the Imperishable One
who does not act.[2]

14

Actions do not
stain me,
nor do I desire

the fruits of actions.
So too, the one
who knows me
is not bound
by actions.

15

Action was undertaken
by the ancient ones
who knew this
and who sought freedom;[3]
so undertake action
as was done
by the ancient ones
in earlier times.

16

Even the poets
are confused by this,
saying, 'What is action?
What is non-action?'
I tell you,
when you know this action,
you will be freed
from impurity.

17

One should have watchful insight
into action,
watchful insight
into wrong action,
and watchful insight
into non-action.
The way of action
is hard to fathom.

18

Among humans,
the person who sees
non-action in action,
and action in non-action,
has insight;
that one undertakes
all actions,
steady in *yoga*.

19

Insightful ones
call that one a pandit
who has winnowed
all aims and desires
from all endeavours
and whose action is burned
in the fire
of wisdom.

20

When one has let go
of clinging
to the fruits of action,
always content
and independent,
even when turning
towards action,
that one does nothing at all.

21

One who is without desire,
but with a self
whose thought is restrained,
and who has left off
all grasping,

undertaking action
with the body alone,
that one does no evil.

22

Content with
accidental gifts,
moving beyond dualities,
free from malice,
the same in fulfilment
and frustration,
even after acting,
that one is not bound.

23

For the one who is free,
whose clinging is gone,
and whose thought
stands firm
in wisdom,
action performed
for sacrifice
dissolves altogether.

24

Brahman is offering;
Brahman is oblation
poured out by Brahman
in the fire of Brahman;
Brahman is attained
by one absorbed
in the action
of Brahman.[4]

25

Some who practise *yoga*
offer sacrifice
only to a god;

others sacrifice
to the sacrifice
with the sacrifice
in the fire
of Brahman.[5]

26

Others offer senses
like hearing
in the fires
of restraint;
others offer sense-objects
like sound
in the fires
of the senses.

27

Some offer
all actions
of the senses
and actions of the breath
into the fire
of the *yoga*
of self-restraint,
lit by wisdom.

28

Some are ascetics
who have sharpened their vows;
they sacrifice
with material things,
or with heated discipline,
or with *yoga*,
or with self-study,
or with wisdom.

29
Some offer the in-breath
in the out-breath.
Others offer the out-breath
in the in-breath.
They hold the paths
of in-breath and out-breath,
focused on deep control
of the breath.

30
Some restrict their food,
and offer breaths
into breaths;
all these knowers
of the sacrifice
have their evil deeds
consumed
by sacrifice.

31
Best of the Kurus,
this world does not belong
to those who do not sacrifice,
much less the other world.
Those who enjoy
nectared remains of sacrifice
go to Brahman,
existent from the beginning.

32
Recognize
that all those many kinds
of sacrifices,
spread out
before Brahman,

are born of action:
when you realize this,
you will be freed.

33

Son of Pritha,
all action
is fully contained
in knowledge:
the sacrifice of knowledge
is better than
the sacrifice of worldly things,
Scorcher of the Enemy.

34

Recognize that
by complete surrender,
by questioning,
by serving,
the wise seers
of truth
will show
wisdom to you.

35

Son of Pandu,
when you know this
you will not again be confused.
Through this,
you will see all beings –
every single one –
in yourself,
and then in me.[6]

36

Even if you are
the most evil
among all

doers of evil,
you will cross beyond
all wickedness
by the boat
of wisdom.[7]

37

Arjuna,
just as the lit fire
makes the kindling
into ashes,
in this same way
the fire of wisdom
makes all actions
into ashes.

38

In this world,
there is no purifier
like wisdom;
in time, one who is
oneself perfected
by *yoga*
finds that wisdom
in the self.

39

With wisdom
as the highest goal,
controlling the senses,
and filled with trust
one reaches wisdom.
Then, with wisdom reached,
one goes quickly
to the highest peace.

40
Without wisdom,
without placing trust,
the doubting self
is destroyed;
there is no pleasure
for the doubting self –
not in this world,
nor in the world beyond.

41
Winner of Wealth,
actions do not bind
the self-possessed one
whose doubt
is severed
by wisdom,
and whose actions
are given up to *yoga*.

42
Son of Bharata,
when, with the knife
of your own wisdom,
you have severed this doubt
that lives in the heart
and begins without wisdom,
then stand up,
and dwell in *yoga*!

THE FIFTH DISCOURSE

Arjuna said:

1

Krishna, you praise
the renunciation
of actions.
Then again, you praise *yoga*.
Which one is better
of these two?
Tell this to me
once and for all.[1]

The Blessed One said:

2

Both renunciation
and the *yoga*
of action
lead to the highest bliss.
But of the two,
the *yoga* of action
is better
than renunciation.

3

Strong-Armed One,
the one who
neither hates nor desires

should be known
as the eternal renouncer –
the one for whom
opposites are the same,
easily freed from bondage.

4

Foolish ones say
samkhya and *yoga*
are separate ideas,
but the pandits don't.
When just one
is practised rightly,
one finds the fruit
of both.

5

Those who practise *yoga*
reach the place
attained by those
who practise *samkhya*.
The one who sees
that *samkhya*
and *yoga* are one
sees rightly.

6

Strong-Armed One,
without *yoga*
renunciation is indeed
hard to achieve;
the sage who
is joined to *yoga*
reaches Brahman
in no time at all.

7

Even when acting,
one is not defiled,
when joined to *yoga*
with a pure self,
a controlled self,
whose senses are conquered,
and whose being
is the self of all beings.

8

When seeing or hearing,
touching or smelling,
eating or walking,
sleeping or breathing,
the one joined to *yoga*,
who knows truth,
thinks, 'I am not doing
anything at all.'

9

Chattering,
letting go, grasping,
opening the eyes,
and shutting the eyes,
that one
holds the thought:
'The senses dwell
in their objects.'

10

Just as a lotus leaf
is not wet by water,
when one has let go
of clinging
and placed actions

in Brahman,
one who acts
is not defiled by evil.

11
When they have let go
of clinging,
those who practise *yoga*
undertake action
to purify the self –
with body, mind
and insight,
even with just the senses.

12
When one has let go
of the fruits of action,
one joined to *yoga*
gains full peace.
The one not joined to *yoga*,
clinging to the fruit,
is bound by actions
of desire.

13
The embodied one
gives up all actions
with the mind,
neither performing
nor causing action,
as a lord
sits contentedly
in the city of nine gates.[2]

14
This master
creates neither agent
nor action

in this world,
nor the linking
of action with its fruit.
But his own nature[3]
keeps on evolving.

15

The one who pervades all
does not take in
the good or harm
done by anyone;
wisdom is covered up
by ignorance,
which confuses
living beings.

16

But among those
whose ignorance
of the self
is destroyed
by wisdom,
their wisdom
illuminates the highest,
like the sun.

17

Those whose insight is that,
whose selves are that,
whose grounding is that,
who hold that as highest,
and whose evils
are shaken off
by wisdom,
do not go to another birth.

18

The pandits see the same –
in a brahmin,
gifted with knowledge
and training,
as in a cow
or in an elephant;
as in a dog,
or in a dog-cooker.[4]

19

Rebirth is conquered
here in this world
by those whose minds
abide in
that sameness;
Brahman has no fault,
and so they abide
in Brahman.

20

When one finds something loved,
one shouldn't be excited;
when one finds something unloved,
one shouldn't tremble.
With insight firm,
without confusion,
knowing Brahman,
one abides in Brahman.

21

The one
who does not cling
to sensations
from the outside,
who finds joy in the self,

and who joins with Brahman
through *yoga*,
reaches endless joy.

22

Son of Kunti,
pleasures
born of sensations
are like wombs filled with pain;
they have a beginning
and an end,
so the wise one
does not rejoice in them.

23

One who can endure
in this world
the shock that begins
in desire and anger,
before release
from the body,
is joined to *yoga*
and a happy person.

24

The one who practises *yoga*,
who has joy within,
delight within,
and then radiance within,
thus reaches cessation[5]
in Brahman,
of one being
with Brahman.

25

The sages
reach cessation
in Brahman;

their evils destroyed,
their dualities cut,
their selves restrained,
they rejoice in the friendship
of all beings.

26

Cessation in Brahman
lies nearby
for those ascetics
who are restrained,
who are not joined
to anger and desire,
who are restrained in thought
and who know the self.

27

Making outside sensation
truly outside,
focusing the eye
between the eyebrows,[6]
making equal
the ingoing breath
and the outgoing breath,
moving in the nose,

28

the sage whose highest path
is release,
whose sense, mind
and insight
are controlled,
whose anger, fear and longing
have disappeared,
is always released.

29

That sage attains peace
who knows me
as the enjoyer
of the heated disciplines
of sacrifice,
as great lord of the whole world,
as one whose heart
is with all beings.

THE SIXTH DISCOURSE

The Blessed One said:

1

The person who does
what must be done,
and does not resort
to the fruit of action,
is a renunciant
and practitioner of *yoga*,
not the one without a fire
and without rituals.

2

Son of Pandu,
know that which
they call renunciation
is *yoga*;
no one becomes
a practitioner of *yoga*
without giving up
purposeful intent.

3

Action is the method
for the sage
wanting to rise
toward *yoga*;
quiet is the method

for the one
who has risen
to *yoga*.

4

The one
who is said
to have risen to *yoga*
is one who has renounced
all purposeful intent,
clinging neither to actions,
nor to the objects
of the senses.

5

One should lift up
the self through the self,
and one should not
make the self sink;
only the self
is friend to the self,
and only the self
is enemy to the self.

6

For the one
who has conquered
the self by the self,
the self is a friend.
For the one who has not,
the self would be
in rivalry,
like an enemy.

7

The highest self
of the victorious one,
the peaceful one,

is composed
in cold and heat,
pleasure and pain,
so also in pride
and disgrace.

8
The practitioner of *yoga*
who is content
with discernment and wisdom,
unmoving, with senses conquered,
to whom a lump of clay,
a stone and a piece of gold
are the same,
is said to be joined to *yoga*.

9
That person is distinguished
who sits apart from friend,
associate and enemy,
who stands with even insight
among the hated
and the loved,
among the righteous,
and the evildoers.

10
A practitioner of *yoga*
should always join
the self to *yoga*,
firm in solitude,
alone and restrained,
in self and thought,
with no desire,
and no possessions.

11
When one sets up
a firm seat,
in a pure place,
neither too high
nor too low,
covered with a cloth,
an antelope skin,
and *kusha* grass,

12
when one directs the mind
to a single point,
actions of the senses
and thoughts controlled,
sitting oneself on the seat,
one should join to *yoga*
in order to purify
the self.

13
One is firm,
unmoving,
holding in balance
the head, neck and body,
looking at the tip
of one's own nose,
not looking in
any one direction.

14
With fear banished,
controlled mind,
and the self peaceful,
firm in the celibate vow
of a student,

thinking of me,
one should sit joined to *yoga*,
with me as highest.

15

Always joining
the self to *yoga*,
the practitioner of *yoga*
who has restrained the mind
goes to
the highest cessation,
and to peace,
standing together with me.[1]

16

Yoga is not about
eating too much,
nor is it about
not eating at all.
It is not about the practice
of sleeping too much,
nor is it about
keeping awake.

17

For one who is
joined to *yoga*,
yoga destroys all pain –
in food and sport,
in the undertaking
of action,
and in sleeping
and awakening.

18

One is said to be
joined in this way,
when one's thought

is restrained;
when one abides
in the self alone,
beyond longing
and all desires.

19

One is like a lit lamp
that does not flicker,
standing without wind.
This likeness is kept in mind
for one who practises *yoga*,
whose thought is controlled,
joined to the *yoga*
of the self.

20

Where thought is at rest,
held back by
the practice of *yoga*,
and where one
is content,
seeing the self
by the self,
in the self,

21

that one knows
the place
of endless joy –
grasped by insight,
beyond the senses,
and when it is firm,
one does not move
away from truth.

22
When one
has reached it,
one can think
of nothing
beyond it;
when one is firm in it,
one is not shaken,
even by deep pain.

23
Let it be known:
this dissolution
of the bond to pain
is called *yoga*;
this *yoga* should be followed
with an absence of doubt,
and with thoughts
that are not despondent.

24
When one has
fully let go
of all those desires
that begin with purpose,
and when one has
wholly reined in
the whole set
of the senses,[2]

25
with insight
firmly grasped,
one should become quiet
little by little.
When one's mind

is fixed on the self,
one should not
think of anything else.

26

From wherever the mind
wanders away,
flitting unsteadily
back and forth,
one should direct it
from that place,
to control
in the self.

27

The practitioner
of *yoga*
who is peaceful in mind,
whose passions
are calm,
without evil,
of one being with Brahman,
reaches the highest joy.

28

The practitioner
of *yoga*,
constantly
restraining the self,
with evil vanished,
reaches endless joy,
easily touching
Brahman.

29

The self of the one
joined to *yoga*
always sees

the same way:
the self is
in all beings
and all beings
are in the self.

30
The one who
sees me everywhere
and sees everything
in me,
I am not lost
to that person,
and that person
is not lost to me.

31
The practitioner of *yoga*
who is devoted to me
as one who abides
in all beings,
abiding in oneness,
in whatever ways
that one is existing,
that one dwells in me.

32
Arjuna,
one who everywhere
sees equality,
through likeness with oneself,
whether pleasure or pain,
is thought to be
the highest practitioner
of *yoga*.

Arjuna said:

33

Killer of Madhu,
because of [the mind's]
instability,
I don't see
the stable foundation
of this *yoga*,
declared by you
with such balance.

34

Krishna,
the mind is ever straying,
troubling,
strong and unyielding;
I think holding it back
is as hard to bring about
as holding back
the wind.

The Blessed One said:

35

Strong-Armed One,
the straying mind,
without doubt,
is hard to hold back –
but by practice
and by not engaging passion,[3]
it is held back,
Son of Kunti.

36

This is what I think:
yoga is hard to reach
for the one whose self

is not restrained,
but it is possible
to reach *yoga*
for one whose self is reined in
by striving in skilful ways.[4]

Arjuna said:

37
One who is not controlled,
but who comes with trust,
whose mind has strayed
from *yoga*,
who has not reached
the fulfilment of *yoga*,
what way does that one
travel, Krishna?

38
Strong-Armed One,
is that one not lost,
like a splintered cloud,
fallen from
both worlds,
without grounding,
confused on the path
of Brahman?

39
Krishna,
You should cut away
this doubt of mine
with nothing left.
No one exists
other than you
who can cut away
this doubt.

The Blessed One said:

40
Son of Pritha,
such a person
is not destroyed –
neither in heaven
nor on earth;
dear friend, no one
who does good
travels the hard road.

41
When one
has reached the worlds
of virtuous action,
and has dwelt for endless years
one who is lost to *yoga*
is then born again
in the home
of the pure and illustrious.

42
Or one exists
in a family
of intelligent
practitioners of *yoga* –
a birth like this
is surely very hard
to reach
in this world.

43
There in that body
one attains
the joining of insight
from the previous body,
and from there,

one strives once again
toward fulfilment,
Joy of the Kurus.

44

One is carried
by the practice
of an earlier life,
even against one's will.
Just the desire
to know *yoga*
goes beyond
the Brahman of the word.

45

Through great effort
and restrained mind,
completely purified
of evil, and fulfilled
through many births,
the practitioner of *yoga*
then travels
the highest way.

46

The practitioner of *yoga*
surpasses those
who practise heated discipline,
and also surpasses those
who are wise,
and those who act in ritual.
Therefore, Arjuna,
be a practitioner of *yoga*!

47

Even among all these
practitioners of *yoga*,
the one who loves me,

who has trust,
and who goes to me
with the inner self,
that one is thought by me
the most closely joined to *yoga*.

You can't do
yoga? Trust in me
and you can

THE SEVENTH DISCOURSE

The Blessed One said:

1

Son of Pritha,
hear this!
With [your] mind
intent on me,
joined to *yoga*,
[your] refuge in me,
in that way you will know me
completely, without doubt.

2

I will explain
this knowledge to you
in its fullness;
as well as the means
of discerning it;
once it is known,
nothing is left to be known
here on earth.

3

Among thousands of mortals,
only some strive
towards fulfilment.
Even among those
who are striving,

and among those
who are fulfilled,
only some truly know me.[1]

4
My material nature[2]
is split
in eight ways:
earth, water,
fire, wind,
space, mind,
insight and
'I'-making.

5
Strong-Armed One,
this is my lower nature.
But be aware
of my other, highest nature –
that nature
being the life by which
this world
is held up.

6
Understand that
all beings
have their origins
in this nature:
I am
the birth
and the dissolution
of the whole world.[3]

7
Winner of Wealth,
there is nothing
higher

than me;
all this
is woven on me,
like patterned jewels
woven on a thread.

8

Son of Kunti,
I am the taste in the waters,
the radiance in the sun
and in the rabbit-marked moon,
the sacred syllable 'Om'[4]
in all the Vedas,
the sound in the air,
and the virility in men.

9

I am the fresh smell
within the earth;
I am the brilliance
in the flaming sun,
and the life in all beings;
and I am
the heated discipline
in those who meditate.

10

Son of Pritha,
recognize me as
the ancient seed of all beings,
there since the beginning.
I am the insight
of the insightful,
the radiance
of those who shine.

11
Bull of the Bharatas,
I am the strength
of the strong;
with neither passion
nor desire,
I am that desire[5]
in beings
to follow *dharma*.

12
Recognize that
the states of being
of *sattva*, *rajas*
and *tamas*
arise from me.
While I am not
in them,
they are in me.

13
This whole world
is confused by
these three states of being
that come from these *guna*s.
It is not aware of me,
the one who is
above all these,
imperishable.

14
The creative power
that comes from these *guna*s
is indeed divine
and hard to master.
Only those who

take refuge in me
can pass beyond
this creative power.

15
The worst of people,
confused evildoers,
do not take refuge in me;
they are attached
to the way of the demon,
and their wisdom
is taken away
through [my] creative power.

16
But Arjuna,
among doers of good,
four kinds honour me:
those who are afflicted;
those who want to know;
those who have a goal;
those who have wisdom,
Bull of the Bharatas.

17
Among them,
the person who has wisdom,
eternally joined to *yoga*,
is distinguished,
devoted to one thing.
I surely love
the one who has wisdom,
and that one also loves me.

18
All of these
are exalted,
but the one with wisdom

is thought to be
my own self;
the one joined to *yoga*
abides in me
as the highest way.

19

At the end
of many births,
the one with wisdom
takes refuge in me,
thinking, 'Vasudeva[6]
is everything.'
Such a larger self
is hard to find.

20

Those whose wisdom
is taken away by
this desire and that desire
take refuge in other gods.
They resort to this observance
and that observance,
reined in by their own
material natures.

21

But if one
desires to worship
any honoured form
with trust,
I will grant
to that person
trust
that is immovable.

22

And one joined to
this trust
who desires to honour
this god,
reaches
one's desires,
as they are
ordained by me.

23

But for those
of small intelligence,
this fruit has a limit.
The ones who worship
those gods
go to the gods.
The ones who choose me
truly go to me.

24

While those who have no insight
think of me
as changed into form,
I am formless.
They don't know
my higher being,
imperishable
and incomparable.

25

But I do not shine for all,
wrapped as I am
in the creative power
of *yoga*.
The confused world

does not perceive me,
as I am – unborn,
and imperishable.[7]

26

Arjuna,
I know those beings
who have crossed over,
as well as those
who exist,
and the ones yet to be.
But no one
knows me.

27

Son of Bharata,
because of the rise
of hatred and desire,
and the confusion
of dualities,
at birth, all beings
end up in delusion,
Scorcher of the Enemy.

28

But those whose
evil deeds have ended,
whose actions are pure,
are freed from
the confusion
of dualities.
Those whose vows are firm
are devoted to me.

29

Those who move
towards freedom
from ageing and death,

resorting to me,
know this Brahman
completely;
they know the highest self,
and the entirety of action.

30

They know me as
the highest being,
the highest god,
the highest sacrifice,
and even at the time
of departure,
they know me,
their thought joined to me.

THE EIGHTH DISCOURSE

Arjuna said:

1

Highest among Beings,
what is this Brahman,
what is the highest self,
what is action?
How is
the highest being declared?
And how is
the highest god spoken of?

2

Killer of Madhu,
how and what
is the highest sacrifice
in this body?
And how, at the time
of departure,[1]
are you known by those
whose selves are restrained?

The Blessed One said:

3

Brahman is
the highest imperishable;
the highest self

is said to be
one's own nature, giving rise
to all states of being;
action is understood
as 'sending forth'.[2]

4

Among the embodied,
the highest being
is finite existence;
the highest god
is the great spirit;
I am the highest sacrifice
here in this body,
Chosen One.

5

And at the end time,
remembering me,
freed from the body,
the one who departs
goes to
my state of being.
There is no doubt
in this matter.

6

Whatever state of being
one remembers,
when, at the end,
one abandons the body,
one goes to that state –
always changed
into that state of being,
Son of Kunti.

7

For this reason,
remember me
at all times,
and fight
with insight and mind
placed on me.
And doubtless,
you will come to me.

8

With thought joined
to the practice of *yoga*,
by turning towards
nothing else,
one goes to the
highest divine spirit,[3]
meditating [on that],
Son of Pritha.

9

One should meditate
on the ancient one,
the poet and ruler,
smaller than the atom,
the supporter of all,
whose shape is unknowable,
and whose colour is the sun,
beyond the dark.[4]

10

At the time of departure,
with a motionless mind,
joined to devotion
through the strength of *yoga*,
after making the breath enter

between the two eyebrows,
one goes to
this divine, highest spirit.

11
I will tell you the path
which ascetics enter,
without passion,
where they follow
a celibate vow,
and desire that which
those who know the Veda
call the infinite.

12
When one has restricted
all the doors [of the body],
and kept closed
the mind in the heart,
and put the breath
in the head,
abiding in
the concentration of *yoga*,

13
when one
has said 'Om',
the Brahman of one syllable,
meditating on me,
one goes forth,
abandons the body,
and then travels
the highest way.

14
Son of Pritha,
for the one whose thought
does not ever go elsewhere,

who eternally
remembers me,
for one who practises *yoga*
always joined [to practice],
I am easy to find.

15
When they come near to me,
those great selves
who have gone
to the highest fulfilment
do not reach
another birth –
that impermanent
place of sorrow.

16
The worlds are
always returning
again to birth,
up to the world of Brahman.
But when one has come near to me,
one does not find
another rebirth,
Son of Kunti.

17
The ones who know
that a day of Brahma
ends at a thousand *yugas*,
and that his night
ends at a thousand *yugas*,
are the ones
who know
the day and the night.[5]

18

At the coming of day,
all those things which have form
come from
that which is formless;
at the coming of night,
they are dissolved at random
into that which is known
as the formless.

19

The great group
of beings is born
again and again,
and dissolved
at the coming of night;
it comes into being again
at the coming of day,
Son of Pritha.

20

But higher than this
is another state of being
which is also formless;
it is higher
than that formless state
existent from the beginning.
And when all beings are lost,
it does not die.

21

It is said that
the imperishable
is unseen;
they call that
the highest way.

When they reach this,
they do not return.
That is my highest abode.

22

Son of Pritha,
this highest being
is reachable
by singular devotion;
all beings
stand within it,
this whole world is woven
through it.

23

Bull of the Bharatas,
I will tell you
the time when
those who practise *yoga*
depart,
and the time
of their returning,
and not returning.

24

In light, fire and day,
or the waxing moon
of the month,
and the six months
of the sun's northern path,
then at that time
the ones who know Brahman
go to Brahman.

25

In night and smoke,
and the darkening moon
of the month,

and the six months
of the sun's southern path,
then reaching lunar light,
the one who practises *yoga*
comes back.

26

These two ways
of light and dark
are thought to be eternal
for the world;
by the first,
one does not come back;
by the other,
one comes back again.[6]

27

Son of Pritha,
knowing these two paths,
the one who practises *yoga*
is not at all confused;
because of this,
Arjuna,
at all times
be joined to *yoga*.

28

Knowing all this,
one who practises *yoga*
moves beyond the pure fruit
fixed in the Vedas,
in sacrifices, in gifts
and in heated discipline;
he goes to the ancient
highest place.

THE NINTH DISCOURSE

The Blessed One said:

1

But this
most hidden secret
I will tell you –
as you are the one
who does not sneer:
knowledge, joined with wisdom
– once you've learned this,
you will be freed from impurity.

2

It is a kingly knowledge,
a kingly secret,
a purifier above all,
promoting *dharma*,
learned right before
your eyes,
undying, and pleasant
to perform.

3

Scorcher of the Enemy,
people who do not
have trust
in this *dharma*
have not reached me;

they are born again
in the way of death
and rebirth.

4

This whole world
is woven through
with me,
in a shape
which is formless;[1]
all beings dwell in me,
while I do not
dwell in them.

5

Yet neither do beings
dwell in me.
Behold, my powerful *yoga*:
bearing beings,
and yet not dwelling
in beings,
my own self
causing them to be.

6

As a great wind,
moving
in all places,
dwells eternally
in the sky,
so all beings
dwell in me.
Think of this.

7

Son of Kunti,
all beings move
into my own substance

at the burning end
of a cycle of ages.
And at the birth
of an age,
I again send them out.

8

Borne up by my own
material nature,
again and again
I send out,
by the power
of material nature,
this whole collection of beings
which is, in itself, powerless.

9

Winner of Wealth,
yet these acts
do not bind me;
I sit,
as one
sitting apart,[2]
not clinging
to these acts.

10

With me as witness,
material nature
gives birth
to the moving and the still;
because of this,
Son of Kunti,
the world evolves
in various ways.

11

When I dwell
in human form,
the confused ones
have contempt for me,
not knowing
my highest nature
as the great lord
of beings.

12

Those thoughtless ones
whose hopes,
actions
and wisdom
are all in vain,
abide in
a fiendish, demonic
and deluded nature.

13

But, Son of Pritha,
those whose selves are great,
abiding in divine nature,
they honour me
with a single mind,
knowing me
as the imperishable one,
the beginning of all beings.

14

Continually
praising me,
striving,
their vows firm,
honouring me

with devotion,
eternally joined [to *yoga*],
they worship.

15

And others,
through the sacrifice
of wisdom,
worship me
as the oneness
which is multiple,
placed in many ways,
facing all sides.

16

I am the intention;
I am the sacrifice;
I am the share of offering;
I am the healing plant;
I am the mantra;
I am also heated butter;
I am fire;
I am the poured oblation.[3]

17

I am the father of the world –
its mother, its arranger
and its grandfather;
I am what is to be known;
the purifier;
the sound 'Om';
the *Rig*, the *Sama*
and the *Yajur Veda*.[4]

18

I am the way,
the bearer, the great lord,
the one who sees.

I am home, and shelter,
the heart's companion.
I am birth, death and sustenance;
I am the house of treasure,
and the eternal seed.

19

I give off heat,
and I am the rain.
I hold back,
and I send out.
I am sweet immortality,
as well as death;
being and non-being,
Arjuna.

20

Those who know the Vedas
and drink Soma,
cleansed of their evils
seek heaven, and offer to me
with sacrifices.
They reach the pure world of Indra,
and enjoy the divine pleasures
of the gods in heaven.[5]

21

When they have enjoyed
the wide realm of heaven,
when their merit is gone,
they enter the mortal realm.
Then, following the *dharma*
of the three Vedas,
they desire their desires.
They get what comes and goes.

22

For beings
who honour me,
who guide their thoughts
to me, and no other,
I bring the secure peace
of *yoga*
to those who are
eternally joined [to *yoga*].

23

Even those
who are devoted
to other gods,
but who sacrifice with trust,
they also sacrifice
to me,
although they do not
sacrifice in the right way.

24

I am indeed
the enjoyer
and the ruler
of all sacrifices.
But they do not
recognize me
in reality,
so they fall.

25

Those who choose gods
go to the gods.
Those who choose ancestors
go to the ancestors.
Those who honour the ghosts

go to the ghosts.
Those who sacrifice to me
go to me.

26

Leaf and blossom,
fruit and water:
from the one who offers
these to me
with devotion,
the one whose self is pure,
I take that offering
of devotion.

27

Son of Kunti,
all that you do,
all that you take,
all that you offer,
all that you give,
all that you strive for,
in heated discipline –[6]
do that in offering to me.

28

You will surely be freed
from the bonds of action
and its fruits,
the pure and impure.
With your self free,
joined to the *yoga*
of renunciation,
you will come to me.

29

I am the same
in all beings.
There is no one

whom I hate or love.
But those who honour me
with devotion,
are within me,
and I am also in them.

30

If the one
who does evil
honours me
and not another,
that one is thought
to be good.
That one has begun
in the right way.

31

That one quickly becomes
the very self of *dharma*,
and enters eternal peace.
Recognize
that no one who is
devoted to me
is ever lost,
Son of Kunti.

32

Son of Pritha,
those who seek refuge in me,
even those
who come from evil wombs,
or women, *vaishya*s,[7]
even *shudra*s,[8]
they, too, go on
the highest path.

33

How much more
the pure brahmins
and the royal sages
are devoted in this way!
When you have reached
this unhappy realm
which perishes,
become devoted to me.

34

With your mind on me,
be devoted to me;
sacrifice to me,
and bow with reverence to me.
Joined in this way,
with me as the highest goal –
you will come to
me alone.

THE TENTH DISCOURSE

The Blessed One said:

1

Strong-Armed One,
listen again
to my highest word
which I will
tell you,
whom I love,
with desire
for your well-being.

2

Neither the great
throngs of gods
nor the great sages
know my origin.
In all ways, I am truly
the beginning
of the gods
and the sages.

3

The one who knows me,
without birth,
without beginning,
the great lord of the world,
is not confused

among mortals;
that one is freed
from all forms of harm.

4

Insight, wisdom,
freedom from confusion,
patience, truth
and self-control;
peacefulness,
pleasure and pain,
arising and passing on,
fear and courage –

5

the many kinds
of states of being
arise from me alone:
not doing harm,
equanimity,
contentment,
heated discipline, giving gifts,
fame and infamy.

6

In ancient times,
the seven great sages[1]
and the four Manus,
ancestors of humans,
and the beings
in this world
had their origins in me,
brought forth by my mind.

7

The one
who really knows
my power and *yoga* –

that one is joined to me
in a *yoga*
that does not waver;
there is no doubt
about this.

8

I am
the origin of all,
and all emerges from me.
When they think in this way,
the insightful ones
who are gifted with
creative contemplation,
are part of me.

9

Those whose thought
is focused on me,
whose breath
goes to me,
who awaken each other,
and speak about me,
become eternally
joyful and delighted.

10

They who are
always joined to *yoga*,
who are part of me,
and filled with kindness,
to them I give
the *yoga* of insight.
By that *yoga*,
they come to me.

11

Since I move
in sympathy with them,
while dwelling
in myself,
I destroy their darkness
born of ignorance
with the bright lamp
of wisdom.

Arjuna said:

12

You are the highest Brahman,
the highest dwelling place,
the highest one
who purifies,
the divine
eternal spirit,
the first unborn god
who pervades all.

13

So all the sages
tell you –
the heavenly sage
Narada, and also
Asita Devala,[2]
and Vyasa.
And now,
you tell me so yourself.

14

Lovely-Haired One,
I believe all
that you say
to me is true.
No one knows your forms –

neither the gods
nor the demons,
Blessed One.

15
Highest of spirits,
cause of beings,
lord of beings,
god of gods,
ruler of the world,
you know your own self
through your self
alone.

16
If you will,
please tell me,
with nothing left out,
the divine forms
of your own self –
the forms by which
you pervade all these realms,
and dwell in them.

17
Yogin,[3]
as I continually
reflect on you,
how might I know you?
And in what different
states of being
can I fathom you,
Blessed One?

18
Mover of Men,
tell me again
in each detail,

about the *yoga*
and the form
of your self.
I never tire
of hearing this nectar.

The Blessed One said:

19
Listen! I will tell you
the heavenly forms
of my self;
I will tell you
the primary ones,
for there is no end
to my extent,
Best of the Kurus.

20
Thick-Haired One,
I am the self.
I dwell as the refuge
of all beings,
and I am also
the beginning,
middle and end
of beings.

21
Among the Adityas,
I am Vishnu.
Among the great lights
I am the sun, shining.
Among storm gods, the Maruts,
I am their chief, Marici.
Among stars of the zodiac,
I am the rabbit-marked moon.[4]

22

Among the Vedas,
I am the Sama chant.
Among the gods,
I am Indra, called Vasava.
Among the powers of sense,
I am the mind.
Among beings,
I am thought.[5]

23

Among the Rudras,
I am Shankara.
Among the Yakshas and Rakshas,
I am Vittesha, lord of wealth.
Among the Vasus,
I am fire, the purifier.
And among the mountains,
I am Meru.[6]

24

Son of Pritha, recognize me
as Brihaspati,
the head of household priests,
the ruler of sacrifice.
Among the chief of armies
I am Skanda.[7]
Among the waters,
I am the ocean.

25

Among great sages,
I am Bhrigu.
Of things that are uttered,
I am the syllable 'Om'.
Among sacrifices,

I am the soft recitation.[8]
Among things that do not move,
I am the Himalaya.

26
Among all the trees,
I am the *ashvattha* fig tree.
Among heavenly sages
I am Narada.
Among the Gandharvas,
I am Chief Citraratha.
Among those who are fulfilled
I am the wise sage, Kapila.[9]

27
Among horses,
I am Indra's Uccaihshravas.
Recognize me
to be born of nectar.
Among great elephants,
I am Indra's Airavata.[10]
And among men,
I am their protector.

28
Among weapons,
I am the thunderbolt.
Among cows,
I am the wish-granting cow.
I am Kandarpa,
who makes progeny.
Among serpents,
I am their king, Vasuki.[11]

29
Among snakes,
I am the endless one.
Among sea creatures,

I am Varuna.
Among ancestors,
I am Aryaman, their chief.
Among those who snuff out [life],
I am Yama, god of death.[12]

30
Among the Daityas,
I am their prince Prahlada.
Among those who count,
I am time itself.
Among the animals,
I am the lion, their Lord.
And among the birds,
I am Vainateya.[13]

31
Among purifiers,
I am the wind.
Among those who bear weapons,
I am Rama.
Among sea monsters,
I am Makara, the crocodile.
Among rivers,
I am Ganges, Jahnu's daughter.[14]

32
Arjuna, among creations,
I am the first, last
and middle.
Among insights,
I am insight into
the highest self.
Among those who speak,
I am discourse.

33

Among imperishable sounds,
I am the letter 'A'.
Among words joined together,
I am the simple link.[15]
I alone
am imperishable time;
I am the arranger,
facing everywhere.

34

I am death,
who seizes all,
and the beginning
of that which will be.
Among female deities,
I am Good Name, Wealth and Speech,
Memory, Intelligence,
Constancy, Endurance.[16]

35

Among chants,
I am the great chant to Indra.
Among metres,
I am the perfect Gayatri.
Among months,
I am Margashirsha.
Among seasons,
I am blossoming spring.[17]

36

Among those who cheat,
I am risk.
Among the brilliant,
I am brilliance.
I am victory;

I am resolve.
Among those who possess the truth,
I am truth.

37
Among the Vrishni people,
I am Krishna Vasudeva.
Among the Pandavas,
I'm Arjuna, winner of wealth.
Among wise ones,
I am the author Vyasa.
Among poets,
I am the poet Ushanas.[18]

38
Among rulers with the sceptre,[19]
I am authority.
Among those who want victory,
I am wise conduct.
Among hidden things,
I am silence.
Among the wise,
I am wisdom.

39
Arjuna,
among all beings,
I am the seed.
There is no creature,
moving
or unmoving,
that would be
without me.

40
Scorcher of the Enemy,
there is no end to
my divine forms.

Here indeed,
example by example,
I have declared this,
the true expanse
of my power.

41

Understand
that whatever
powerful being there is –
be it splendid,
or filled with vigour,
it comes to be
from only a small part
of my brilliance.

42

But what, Arjuna,
is the purpose
of this abundant wisdom
to you?
I stand, holding up
this entire world
with only a small part
of my self.

THE ELEVENTH DISCOURSE

Arjuna said:

1

In kindness to me,
you have uttered
the highest mystery,
recognized as
the highest self.
With your words,
my confusion
is gone.

2

Lotus-Eyed One,
I have heard
from you in detail
of two things:
the beginning
and end of beings,
and also your
imperishable greatness.

3

Supreme Lord,
thus it is as
you yourself
say it.
Now I want

to see
your lordly form,
Highest Spirit.

4
Master, Lord of Yoga,
if you think
I am able
to see this,
then show yourself
to me,
you who are
the imperishable one.

The Blessed One said:

5
Son of Pritha,
see my divine forms,
a hundred,
a thousand kinds –
all different,
all divine,
and in many colours
and shapes.

6
See the Adityas,
the Vasus, the Rudras,
the twin Ashvins,
and the Maruts –[1]
these many wonders
which have never
been seen before,
Son of Bharata.

7

See now the whole world,
with all things
moving and unmoving
standing together
in my body,
and anything else
you would like to see,
Thick-Haired One.

8

But you are
not able
to see
with your own eye,
so I will
give to you
the divine eye;[2]
see my powerful *yoga*.

Sanjaya said:

9

Your Majesty,
when he said this,
Hari, the great lord
of *yoga*,
showed to Arjuna
the Son of Pritha
his highest,
most powerful, form.

10

It had many
mouths and eyes;
many wondrous
aspects to behold;
many divine ornaments;

many divine weapons
of war,
raised high.

11

Bearing divine
garlands and garments,
divine scents
and oils,
the god held
every wonder –
facing everywhere,
without end.

12

If a thousand suns
had risen
in the sky
all at once,
such brilliance
would be
the brilliance
of that great self.[3]

13

There, Arjuna,
the son of Pandu, saw
in the body
of the God of gods
the whole world,
standing as one,
and yet divided up
in many ways.

14

Then Arjuna,
winner of wealth,
was seized by awe;

his hair stood on end.
Bowing, with folded hands,
with his head bent
towards the god,
he said:

Arjuna said:

15

I see the gods
in your body,
and all kinds of beings
gathered together:
Lord Brahma, seated
in a lotus,
all the sages
and all the divine serpents.[4]

16

I see you everywhere:
arms, bellies, faces, eyes –
form without end.
I see you,
Lord of the Universe,
Manifold One,
you have no beginning,
no middle, no end.

17

I see you,
who are hard to see,
completely, beyond measure.
With the light of a sun
whose fire is blazing,
you shine everywhere –
a mountain of light,
with crown, club and discus.[5]

18

You are to be known
as the highest, unchanging;
you are the great refuge of all,
you are the imperishable,
eternal protector
of *dharma*.
I know your spirit
to be ancient.

19

I see you,
with endless vital power,
endless arms,
eyes of the sun and moon,
your mouth taking in
fiery offerings,
scorching all this world
with your own light.

20

This realm
between earth and sky
is filled by you
at every point;
when the three worlds see
your wondrous and awful form,
they start to tremble,
Great Self.

21

There, great gatherings
of gods enter you.
Some sing praise,
fearful, with folded hands.
When the gatherings

of fulfilled beings
and great sages say, 'Svasti!'
they praise you with many songs.

22

They all see you, truly amazed:
the Rudras, the Adityas,
the Vasus, and the Sadhyas;
the All-gods; the two Ashvins;
the Maruts; the Drinkers of Steam;
the groups of Gandharvas,
the Yakshas, the Demons,
and those who are fulfilled.[6]

23

Strong-Armed One,
when the worlds
see your great form,
with many eyes and mouths,
many arms, thighs and feet,
with many fearsome tusks
and many bellies,
they tremble as I do.

24

Vishnu, since I have seen you
ablaze with many colours,
touching the sky,
flames in your huge eyes,
your mouth gaping,
my self trembles
and I find neither
courage nor calm.[7]

25

Show compassion, Lord of Gods,
Abode of the World!
When I have seen your faces

with many fearsome tusks,
so much like the fires
at the end of time,
I do not know the way,
and I find no refuge.

26

And all these sons
of Dhritarashtra,
alongside the gatherings
of kings Bhishma, Drona
and Karna,
son of the charioteer,
together with our
chief warriors, too,

27

all in a rush,
they enter
your terrible mouths,
gaping with tusks.
Some appear
with heads crushed,
clinging between
your teeth.

28

The heroes
of the mortal world
enter your flaming mouths,
as so many
currents of water
in a river
might run
towards the ocean.

29

As moths[8]
that fly
to their full
will rush to death
in the blazing fire,
so, too, worlds
rush to death
in your mouths.

30

Vishnu,
your mouths,
their flames licking the worlds,
devour on all sides.
Your fierce rays
burn the earth,
even as they fill it
with light.[9]

31

Tell me who you are
in your terrible form.
May you be honoured,
Chosen of the Gods.
Show compassion!
I want to know you, Primal One;
I do not understand
your activity.

The Blessed One said:

32

I am time that has aged,
who makes the world perish.
I have come forth
to destroy the worlds.
Even without you,

these warriors
facing off against each other
will no longer exist.

33

So stand up, and gain honour!
After conquering enemies,
enjoy an abundant reign.
I've already destroyed them.
You who sling arrows
from the left and the right,
be an instrument,
and nothing more.

34

All these heroes of battle,
Drona, Bhishma,
Jayadratha and Karna,
have been struck down by me.
Do not be troubled, but strike!
Fight! For you will
conquer enemies
in battle.

Sanjaya said:

35

When he heard
the words of
the lovely-haired god,
Arjuna, trembling
despite his kingly crown,
his hands folded, fearful,
and bowing down,
spoke to Krishna again.

Arjuna said:

36
Bristling-Haired One,
it is right that the world
exults, delighting in your fame;
that the demons are fearful,
and flee all places;
and that the gatherings
of fulfilled beings
honour you.

37
And why, Great Self,
would they not bow
to you, the first maker?
endless lord of gods,
greater than Brahma,
abode of the world,
undying, existent,
non-existent, and yet beyond.

38
You are the highest abode
of all the universe,
the god in the beginning,
the spirit of old,
You are the knower,
and that which is to be known.
All is pervaded by you,
One of Endless Form!

39
You are Vayu, Yama,[10]
Agni, Varuna,
the rabbit-marked moon,
the lord of creatures,
the first great-grandfather.

May honour be made to you
a thousand times, and yet again.
Honour to you!

40

Honour to you,
before you and behind you;
honour to you on all sides!
You who are all,
you are force without measure,
endless courage.
Since you reach all,
you are all.

41

I was in ignorance
about your majesty
when I said hastily
'O Krishna of the Yadu,
O Friend!'
I was thinking
as a friend would –
in confusion, and also love.

42

If you were badly treated,
in jest, eating or sitting,
lying in bed or in play,
alone or even
in front of others,
I ask your pardon,
Immeasurable,
Unshakeable One!

43

You are father of the world,
of the moving and the still –
its weighty, honoured teacher.

There is no one like you
in the three worlds.
How can there be another
who is greater,
Incomparable One?

44

Thus bowing
with body laid down,
I ask your mercy,
Praiseworthy Lord.
Have patience, God,
as a father for a son,
or a friend for a friend,
a lover for a beloved.

45

I have seen what has
never before been seen.
I am filled with delight;
my mind is shaken with fear.
God, let me see the form [I know]!
Lord of Gods,
Abode of the Earth,
show compassion.

46

I would like to see you
in that form,
with crown and club
and discus in hand.
Thousand-Armed One,
One Who has All Shapes,
take on that
four-armed form!

The Blessed Lord said:

47
Arjuna,
in favour to you,
I showed this highest form
through my own *yoga*.
No one other than you
has seen this before;
it is made of light,
endless, primordial.

48
Neither by Vedic study
nor Vedic sacrifice,
nor ritual actions, nor gifts,
nor heated disciplines,
can I be seen in this form
in the human realm
by anyone other than
you, Brave Kuru.

49
So do not tremble
and do not be confused;
you have seen
my awe-inspiring form,
and your dread disappeared,
your mind encouraged.
See again this form of mine
[that you know].

Sanjaya said:

50
After he spoke to Arjuna,
the son of Vasudeva
showed his own form again,

and he calmed
Arjuna's dread
when the great self once again
took on a pleasing,
gentle appearance.

Arjuna said:

51
Mover of Men,
as I see this,
your gentle
human form,
I am now
composed.
My thoughts have returned
to a natural state.

The Blessed One said:

52
The form of mine
which you have seen
is hard to discern.
Even the gods
are eternally
wanting to have
the sacred sight
of this form.

53
Neither through Veda,
nor heated discipline,
nor gift,
nor sacrifice,
is it possible

to see me
in the way
you have seen me.

54

Arjuna,
I can only be known
by devotion that has
no other object.
In this way,
may I be truly known
and seen and reached,
Scorcher of the Enemy.

55

The one who acts on my behalf,
who holds me as highest,
who is devoted to me,
who lets go of clinging
and is free from hatred
towards all beings,
comes to me,
Son of Pandu.

THE TWELFTH DISCOURSE

Arjuna said:

1

Between the ones who are
always joined to *yoga*,
and honour you with devotion,
and the ones who honour
the imperishable one,
the one without form,
who is the wisest
about *yoga*?

The Blessed One said:

2

Those who are
eternally joined to *yoga*,
and who honour me
with the mind fixed on me,
and gifted with
the highest trust,
I think of them
as the most joined to *yoga*.

3

But those who honour
the imperishable one,
who is undefinable,

and without form,
who pervades all
and is beyond thought,
unmoving, steady,
as if fixed on a mountaintop,

4

and those whose many senses
are reined in together,
with equal insight
in all places,
and who exult
in the good
of all beings,
also reach me.

5

The pain of those
whose thought focuses on
the one without form
is greater.
The goal of the
one without form
is hard to reach
for those with bodies.

6

But those
who give up
all actions to me,
who hold me as highest,
and with *yoga*
where the goal is clear,
in pure concentration,
they honour me.[1]

7

Son of Pritha,
for those whose thoughts
have entered
into me,
I will very soon become
their uplifter
from the ocean
of death and rebirth.

8

Place your mind
on me alone;
let your power
of insight
enter into me.
Then doubtless,
from now on,
you will abide in me.

9

If you cannot
put your thought
steadily on me,
then you should seek
to reach me
through the practice
of *yoga*,
Winner of Wealth.

10

If you are not able
even to practise,
then be focused
on my work.
Also, while doing

actions for my sake,
you will reach
fulfilment.

11

Or, if you are unable
to do even this,
take refuge
in my power,
leaving aside
all fruit of action.
Act from that place,
holding back the self.

12

Wisdom is better
than practice,
and focused mind
is better than wisdom.
Letting go of
the fruit of action
is better than focused mind.
From letting go, peace soon comes.

13

One who has no hatred
for any being,
a compassionate friend,
without the sense of 'mine',
without making an 'I',
one who is patient,
for whom pain and pleasure
are the same,

14

that practitioner of *yoga*
who is always content,
whose self is controlled,

and whose resolve is firm,
whose power of insight
and mind are fixed on me,
who is devoted to me,
that one is dear to me.[2]

15

The one in whose presence
the world does not tremble,
and who does not tremble
in the presence of the world,
who is free
from pleasure and impatience,
fear and anxiety,
is also dear to me.

16

The one who is
able, pure and impartial,
who sits apart,
whose anxiety is gone,
who leaves off
all endeavours,
who is devoted to me,
is dear to me.

17

The one who
neither rejoices
nor resents,
neither sorrows nor lusts,
letting go of states
both happy and unhappy,
filled with devotion,
is dear to me.

18

The one for whom
enemy and friend,
honour and infamy,
cold and heat,
pleasure and pain,
are the same,
who has moved away
from clinging,

19

the one for whom
curse and praise are equal,
who keeps silent,
content with whatsoever
comes his way,
without home, with steady mind,
full of devotion,
that one is dear to me.

20

Those who honour
that nectar of *dharma*
spoken in this way,
holding trust,
holding me
as highest,
devoted to me,
are very dear to me.

THE THIRTEENTH DISCOURSE

Arjuna said:

Lovely-Haired One,
I want to know
matter and spirit;
the sacred ground,
and those who know
the sacred ground;
wisdom,
and the object of wisdom.[1]

The Blessed One said:

1

Son of Kunti,
this body
is the sacred ground.
The wise ones say
the one who knows this
is the one called
the knower
of the sacred ground.[2]

2

Son of Bharata,
recognize also
that I am the one
who knows the sacred ground

in all sacred grounds.
Knowledge of [both] sacred ground
and the knower of sacred ground –
that I consider wisdom.

3

Hear from me in brief
what this sacred ground is
and what its nature is;
what its transformations are
and where they arise from;
hear also
who the knower is
and the knower's power.

4

Chanted by the sages,
in many ways,
one by one,
with various metres,
with thread-like verses,[3]
focusing on Brahman,
and reasoned through
decisively.

5

The gross elements,
the awareness of 'I',
the power of insight,
and that beyond form;
the eleven powers
of sense;
and the five arenas
where the senses act;[4]

6
desire, hatred,
pleasure and pain,
the whole body,
the power of thought,
and of firmness:
this is the sacred ground
explained in brief,
with its examples.

7
Absence of arrogance,
absence of deceit,
absence of harm,
patience and virtue,
sitting with one's teacher,
purity, steadiness,
and the restraint
of the self;

8
indifference
to the objects of sense;
and the absence
of awareness of 'I';
holding in mind
the wrongs of pain,
illness, old age,
birth and death;

9
absence of clinging,
absence of grasping
to things, such as
home, wife and child;
and eternally with thoughts

which are even-minded
towards desired
and undesired events;

10

not fond
of crowds of people,
resorting to
a place apart,
without straying
from devotion to me,
and with no other
form of *yoga*;

11

being eternally
in the wisdom
of the supreme self,
holding in mind the aim
of the wisdom of truth:
this is declared as true wisdom,
and its contrary
is ignorance.

12

I will tell you
what should be known;
and knowing it,
one gains immortality.
It is the highest Brahman,
without beginning,
said to be neither being
nor non-being.

13

This has a hand and foot
in all places,
and an eye, face and head

in all places.
In the world,
it has hearing in all places;
it is present,
pervading all.[5]

14

It has the semblance
of all the *gunas*,
yet it is turned away
from the senses.
It does not cling,
and yet bears all.
It has no *gunas*
and yet partakes of them.

15

It is both inside
and outside beings,
moving and unmoving.
It is not to be
comprehended
because of its subtlety;
it stands far off
and also nearby.

16

Among beings,
it is not separate,
yet it stands
as if separated,
and should be known
as the bearer of beings.
It is the absorber
and creator.

17

It is said, too,
to be the light of lights;
it is said to be
beyond darkness;
it is known as wisdom
and the goal of wisdom.
It is seated
in the heart of all.

18

This is the sacred ground,
and the wisdom,
and the object of wisdom,
briefly spoken.
When one who is
devoted to me
comprehends this, that one
enters my state of being.

19

Recognize, too,
that both
spirit and matter
are without beginning.
And recognize that
the transformations
and *guna*s
arise from matter.

20

'Matter'[6] is said to be
the reason
for the agency
of cause and effect.
and 'spirit' is said to be

the reason
for the experience
of pleasure and pain.

21

Spirit abides
in matter
and partakes of the *gunas*,
born of matter.
Clinging to the *gunas*,
it is the cause
of its birth in wombs,
of being and non-being.[7]

22

The highest spirit
in this body
is also called
the highest self,
the great lord,
the one who partakes,
who supports, who approves
and who observes.[8]

23

The one who
recognizes
matter and spirit,
together with the *gunas*,
is not ever
born again,
no matter what way
one already exists.

24

Some see the self
in the self,
through the self,

by meditation.
Others see it
through the *yoga* of *samkhya*.
And others see it
through the *yoga* of action.[9]

25

But some do not
know in this way,
and when they have
heard from others,
they worship,
and also cross
beyond death, devoted to
that revelation.[10]

26

Bull of the Bharatas,
recognize that
when any being,
moving or still, is born,
it is from the union
of the sacred ground
and the one who knows
the sacred ground.[11]

27

The one
who sees
the highest lord,
abiding alike
in all beings,
not dying
even as they die,
that one truly sees.

28

Seeing the same lord
existing everywhere,
that one does not
do harm
to the self
through the self;
that one then goes along
the highest way.[12]

29

One who sees
all actions
done wholly
by means of matter,
and that
one's own self
is not the agent,
that one sees clearly.

30

When one sees
the multiplicity
of states of being
abiding in one,
and spreading out
from that one alone,
one then arrives
at Brahman.

31

Son of Kunti,
because this highest,
imperishable self
has no beginning,
and no *guna*s,

it neither acts nor is stained,
even though abiding
in the body.

32

Just as space
pervades all, and yet
because of its subtlety
is not stained,
everywhere the self,
while abiding
in the body,
is not stained.[13]

33

Son of Bharata,
as a single sun
lights up
this whole realm,
so, too, the one who dwells
in the sacred ground[14]
lights up
this whole sacred ground.

34

The ones who know
through the eye of wisdom
the difference
between sacred ground
and the knower of sacred ground,
and the freedom
of matter from being,
they go to the highest.

THE FOURTEENTH DISCOURSE

The Blessed One said:

1
I will tell you again
the highest wisdom;
when the sages
came to know
this utmost wisdom,
they went
from here
to the highest fulfilment.

2
After they have arrived
at this wisdom,
the same essence
as myself,
they do not come into being
at the creation,
nor do they tremble
at the dissolution.

3
Son of Bharata,
the great Brahman
is my womb;
in this I place
the embryo.

From that emerges
the origin
of all beings.[1]

4
Son of Kunti,
Brahman is
the great womb
of all forms
that exist;
I am the father
who places
the seeds.[2]

5
Strong-Armed One,
sattva, *rajas*
and *tamas*
are *guna*s
born of matter;
they bind the embodied,
imperishable one
within the body.[3]

6
Blameless One,
there *sattva* is
stainless
and brings light;
it binds by connection
to joy,
and by connection
to wisdom.

7
Son of Kunti,
recognize that *rajas*
has the nature of passion

arising from
connection to thirst;
it binds this embodied one
through connection
to action.

8

Son of Bharata,
recognize that *tamas*
is born of ignorance,
and is the confusion
of all embodied ones;
it binds
through sleep, laziness
and distraction.

9

Son of Bharata,
sattva brings
connection to joy;
rajas brings
connection to action;
tamas brings
connection to neglect,
and obscures wisdom.

10

Son of Bharata,
sattva ascends
when it prevails
over *rajas* and *tamas*;
rajas can prevail
over *sattva* and *tamas*;
tamas can prevail
over *sattva* and *rajas*.

11
When a light
is born
in all doorways
of this body,
and when wisdom occurs,
then one should know
that *sattva*
has grown strong.

12
Bull of the Bharatas,
greed, exertion,
the beginning
of action,
restlessness and lust
are born
when *rajas*
has grown strong.

13
Son of Kuru,
absence of light,
absence of exertion,
neglect,
and confusion
are born
when *tamas*
has grown strong.

14
When *sattva*
has grown strong,
the embodied one
goes to dissolution;
then one enters

the stainless realms
of those who know
the highest.

15

When [at death] one dissolves
in *rajas*, one is born
among those
clinging to action;
when [at death] one dissolves
in *tamas*, one is born
in the wombs
of the deluded.[4]

16

They say that
action well done
has fruit without stain,
filled with *sattva*;
but the fruit
of *rajas* is pain,
and the fruit
of *tamas* is ignorance.

17

From *sattva*,
wisdom is born,
and from *rajas*,
greed is born;
neglect,
confusion
and ignorance
arise from *tamas*.

18

The ones who abide
in *sattva* rise up;
the ones who have *rajas*

abide in the middle;
the ones who abide
in the lowest *guna* state,
those who have *tamas*,
go downward.

19

When the one
who observes
perceives an agent
which is not separate
from the *guna*s,
and knows the element
higher than the *guna*s,
that one reaches my being.

20

When the embodied one
transcends these three *guna*s
which come into being
in the body,
that one reaches
eternity, and is free
from sorrow, old age,
death and birth.

Arjuna said:

21

Splendid One,
does one who has transcended
the three *guna*s
have special marks
and practice?
And how does
one transcend
the three *guna*s?

The Blessed One said:

22

Son of Pandu,
that one does not hate
occurrences
of confusion,
or of exertion,
or of brightness;
nor does that one desire
that they not occur.

23

One who stands firm,
and does not stir,
one who is seated
as if sitting apart,[5]
who is not shaken
by the *guna*s,
but thinks
'The *guna*s are turning';

24

one who is self-contained;
for whom pleasure and pain
are the same,
as are a lump of earth,
a stone and a piece of gold;
one who is steady,
for whom the loved and unloved
are equal, as are praise and blame;

25

the one for whom
honour and dishonour
are equal;
as are friend and enemy;
who abandons all

endeavours;
that one is said
to transcend the *guna*s.

26

And the one
who serves me
with the *yoga* of devotion,
and does not waver,
that one transcends the *guna*s
and becomes ready
for becoming one
with Brahman.[6]

27

I am the support
of Brahman,
the immortal
and imperishable;
and the support
of everlasting *dharma*;
and the support
of unique joy.

THE FIFTEENTH DISCOURSE

The Blessed One said:

1

They say
the *ashvattha* tree
is imperishable,
its roots high,
its branches below.
The metres are its leaves;
the one who knows this
is wise in the Veda.[1]

2

Its branches spread wide
below and above,
grown large through the *guna*s,
it sprouts the objects
of sense;
its roots are stretched below,
growing action
in the human realm.

3

The form of the *ashvattha*
is not to be discerned here,
neither its end,
nor beginning,
nor ongoing life.

When its fully grown roots
are cut by the strong axe
of non-clinging,[2]

4

then that place must be sought
where, once they have gone,
they will not turn back again,
and they think,
'I take refuge
in that first spirit
where activity flowed forth
in ancient times.'

5

Without pride or confusion,
the wrongs of clinging vanquished,
eternal in the highest self,
desires turned away,
freed from dualities
of pleasure and pain,
those who are not confused go
to that imperishable place.[3]

6

Neither the sun
nor the rabbit-marked moon
nor flame
lights up
that place;
when they have gone
to my highest dwelling place,
they do not return.

7

Just a fragment of me
in the realm of the living
is the eternal

individual life;
it draws to itself
the senses dwelling
in material nature,
and the sixth [sense] is the mind.[4]

8

When the lord[5]
gains a body,
and when he leaves it,
he goes and takes up
the senses,
just as the wind
takes fragrances
from the place where they began.

9

This lord rules
taste and smell,
hearing, sight
and touch,
as well as the mind;
he enjoys
the objects
of the senses.

10

The confused
do not perceive the lord
as he leaves or stays,
or partakes
in the midst of the *gunas*,
but the ones
with eyes of wisdom
see him.

11

In their effort,
the practitioners of *yoga*
see this one
abiding in the self,
but even with effort
those thoughtless ones
whose selves are not prepared,
do not see him.

12

The brilliance
which comes from the sun
lights up the world
with no break;
it is in the moon,
and in fire;
recognize that brilliance
as mine.

13

When I enter the earth
on which all creatures walk,
I preserve all beings
with energy.
When I become Soma,[6]
liquid in nature,
I cause the plants
to flower.

14

When I become that fire
which belongs to all people,
and enter the body
of all who breathe,
I have joined

the in-breath
with the out-breath,
and I cook four kinds of food.

15
I am seated in the heart of all;
memory, wisdom and reason
come from me.
I am especially
to be known through the Vedas,
as I am a knower of Veda
and the creator
of Vedanta.

16
In the world,
there are two spirits;
one can be destroyed,
and the other
can never be destroyed.
All beings can be destroyed,
but the one who stands above all
is called the indestructible.

17
But the highest spirit
is other than this;
it is called
the highest self,
and when it enters
the three worlds,
it holds them up
as the imperishable lord.

18
Since I go beyond
that which is destroyed
and am higher even

than the indestructible,
I am known
as the highest self –
in the world
and in the Veda.

19

Son of Bharata,
the one who
is not confused
recognizes me
as the highest spirit;
recognizing all, that one
is devoted to me
with fullness of being.

20

Blameless One,
Son of Bharata,
this most secret rule
is told by me,
and when one has awakened,
one would be
filled with insight,
and finished with one's task.

THE SIXTEENTH DISCOURSE

The Blessed One said:

1

Purity in truth;
being without fear;
abiding in the *yoga*
of wisdom;
sacrifice, self-control
and charity;
the right path, heated discipline
and study of the Vedas;

2

absence of harm;
truthfulness;
absence of anger;
renunciation and peace;
avoidance of slander;
compassion for beings;
freedom from lust, kindness,
modesty and discretion;

3

Son of Bharata,
energy, patience,
courage and purity;
absence of hatred;
moderation in honour:

these are the traits
of those born
to the divine condition.

4

Son of Pritha,
fraud, insolence
and hostile conceit;
anger, rough speech too,
and ignorance;
these are the traits
of those born
to the demonic condition.

5

The divine condition
leads to freedom,
and the demonic condition
leads to bondage.
Do not be sorrowful;
you are born
to the divine condition,
Son of Pandu.

6

In this realm,
there are created
two kinds of beings:
divine and demonic.
The divine has been told
in detail; now hear from me
about the demonic,
Son of Pritha.

7

Demonic men
recognize
neither exertion,

nor its cessation,
neither purity
nor even good action.
There is no truth
found in them.

8

They do not have truth,
and have no place to stand.
They say that
the earth is godless,
not created
in causal succession.
How else is it caused? They say:
'It is caused by desire!'[1]

9

Supporting this view,
those whose selves are lost,
whose insight is narrow
and whose actions are cruel
come into being
as enemies
bent on the destruction
of the world.

10

Dependent on desire
which is hard to satisfy,
steeped in fraud, pride
and drunkenness,
they have grasped false ideas
through confusion,
and move ahead
with impure vows.

11

With no end
of anxious thoughts,
clinging to an end
which is dissolution,
their highest goal
is the enjoyment
of desire.
Without a doubt of [their] truth,

12

they are bound
by a hundred snares of hope;
their highest goals
are anger and desire;
they seek hoards of wealth
in mistaken ways,
for the enjoyment
of desire.

13

'This has been gained
by me today!
And I will get this desire –
a desire
which carries the mind
like a chariot.[2]
This wealth is also mine,
and so will this be mine!

14

This enemy
has been struck down by me,
and I will strike
others too!
I am the lord,

the one who enjoys,
fulfilled, strong
and happy.

15

I am rich
and well born;
who else is there like me?
I will sacrifice;
I will give;
I will be joyful!'
Thus say those
confused by ignorance.

16

Wandering away
with many thoughts,
they are covered
by a net of confusion.
Clinging to
the enjoyment of desire,
they fall into
an impure hell.

17

Immovable,
self-absorbed,
accompanied by lust,
pride and wealth,
they sacrifice
in name only,
fraudulently,
and without Vedic rules.[3]

18

They cling to
anger and desire,
arrogance and force,

and 'I'-making;
those who grumble
in this way hate me,
whether in their own
or another's body.

19

In cycles of rebirth,
over and over,
I throw the impure,
wretched people,
cruel and
filled with hate,
into the wombs
of demons.

20

Son of Kunti,
when they have entered
the demon womb,
they are deluded
birth after birth.
They do not reach me,
and then they travel
on the lowest way.

21

This is the threefold
gate of hell,
which destroys the self.
Therefore,
one should let go
the threefold group
of greed, anger
and desire.[4]

22
Son of Kunti,
when one is freed
from the three
gates of dark *tamas*,
one proceeds
in the best way for the self.
Thus one goes
on the highest way.

23
The one who lets go
of the rule of Vedic law
and exists according to
his own desires,
reaches neither
fulfilment
nor happiness
nor the highest way.

24
Thus, following
Vedic law,
which focuses on
that to be done
and not to be done,
and knowing Vedic law,
you should perform action
here in this world.

THE SEVENTEENTH DISCOURSE

Arjuna said:

1

Krishna,
what is the place
of those who let go
of the rule of Vedic law,
but who sacrifice
filled with trust?[1]
Is it *sattva*,
or *rajas* or *tamas*?

The Blessed One said:

2

There are three kinds
of trust;
it is born
of one's own nature.
Listen to this:
it can be sattvic,
or rajasic,
or tamasic.

3

Son of Bharata,
trust follows
the truth

of each *guna*.
Humans are made
of trust;
they grow to become
whatever they trust.

4

The sattvic people
sacrifice to gods,
and the rajasic ones
to demons and yakshas.
The others,
the tamasic ones,
sacrifice to the dead
and gangs of ghosts.

5

People who undergo
fierce, heated disciplines,
not ordained
by Vedic law,
joined to
'I'-making and fraud,
together with force,
rage and desire –[2]

6

recognize these
as demonic in intent,
thoughtlessly harming
the multitude
of elements
in the body,
and also harming me,
who exists in the body.

7
Food is also dear
to everyone
in three ways:
as sacrifice, as heat
and also as gift.
Hear now
the difference
between them.

8
The foods that
increase satisfaction,
pleasure, health, strength,
truth and long life,
that are flavourful, smooth,
firm and pleasant,
are dear
to the sattvic.

9
Foods that are
hot, salty and sour,
sharp, burning, rough
and fiery,
are desired
by the rajasic,
yielding disease,
grief and sorrow.

10
Food that is
dear to the tamasic
is not fit
for sacrifice;
it is a leftover,
and stale,

stinking, tasteless
and spoiled.

11

Sacrifice is sattvic
when offered
according to Vedic law
by those who
desire no fruit,
and who focus the mind
on that which is
to be sacrificed.

12

But recognize that
sacrifice is rajasic
when it is offered
with the fruit
held in mind,
and also offered
toward a fraudulent end,
Best of the Bharatas.

13

People see as tamasic
a sacrifice given
without confidence,
without sponsorship,
the mantras thrown away,
the food not offered
and Vedic law
disparaged.

14

Honouring the gods,
twice-born teachers
and people of wisdom;

purity, virtue,
chastity and
absence of harm, are said
to be the heated discipline
of the body.

15

Speech that
does not cause distress,
that is truthful, pleasant
and beneficial,
and the practice
of Vedic study, are said
to be the heated discipline
of the word.

16

Clarity of mind,
gentleness,
self-control,
silence
and purity of being
are said to be
the heated discipline
of the mind.

17

They regard this
threefold heated discipline
as sattvic
when it is practised
with the highest trust
by those who are
joined to *yoga*
and desire no fruit.

18

That heated discipline
is said to be
rajasic,
wavering and unfixed,
when it is done
fraudulently,
with the purpose of honour,
respect and favour.

19

That heated discpline
is said to be tamasic
when it is done
with torment,
with self-deluded ideas,
or with the purpose
of destroying
another being.

20

That gift given to one
who has not done
a previous favour,
and only with the thought
'This is to be given',
in the right time and place,
and to the right person,
that gift is known as sattvic.

21

But that given
with the purpose of reward,
or with regard
to the fruit,
and that given
unwillingly,

that gift is known
as rajasic.

22

And that gift given
at the wrong place and time,
and to the wrong person,
without the proper decorum
of ritual,
and with disrespect,
that gift is said
to be tamasic.

23

Thus, the *Om tat sat*[3]
is known as the threefold
designation of Brahman.
In ancient times,
the brahmins,
the sacrifices
and the Vedas
were arranged in this way.

24

When sacrifice, gifts
and acts of heated discipline
are begun,
then 'Om' is uttered
by those who speak
of Brahman,
as is told
by Vedic law.

25

Saying '*tat*'
without interest
in their fruits,

acts of heated discipline,
and sacrifice,
and different acts of giving,
are performed by those
who desire freedom.

26

'*Sat*' is said
in its meaning
of true reality
and real goodness;
thus the word '*sat*'
is also used
for a worthy act,
Son of Pritha.

27

In sacrifice,
in heated discipline
and in giving,
sat is also called
'being steadfast',
and action which has this end
is also shown
to be *sat*.

28

Oblation given,
or heated discipline
undertaken without trust,
is called *asat*.
That is not for us –
neither here,
nor after death,
Son of Pritha.

THE EIGHTEENTH DISCOURSE

Arjuna said:

1

Strong-Armed One,
I want to know,
taking each one by itself,
the way it really is,
first, in renunciation,
and then, in letting go,
Bristling-Haired One,
Killer of Keshin.[1]

The Blessed One said:

2

The poets know
that the leaving aside
of action based on desire
is renunciation;
and the clear-sighted see
that the giving up
of all fruit of such action
is called letting go.

3

Some who are wise
say that action is full of wrong,
and should be let go;

and others say that
action made up of
heated discipline,
giving and sacrifice
should not be let go.

4

Best of the Bharatas,
hear my final thought
about this question of
letting go.
Letting go
is also well known
as threefold,
Tiger among Men.

5

Acts of heated discipline,
giving and sacrifice
are not to be let go,
but rather carried out;
for heated discipline,
giving and sacrifice
are purifiers
of the wise.

6

But, Son of Pritha,
these very actions
are to be carried out
after one has let go
of clinging
to the fruits;
this is without a doubt
my highest thought.

7

But renunciation
of prescribed action
is not fitting;
the letting go
of such action
is said to be tamasic
and arises
from confusion.

8

The one who lets go
of an action
because of difficulty,
or fear of bodily pain,
thus carries out letting go
in a rajasic way,
and will not attain
the fruit of that letting go.

9

Arjuna,
when prescribed action
is carried out because it is
simply to be done,
when one has let go
of clinging to the fruit,
this letting go
is thought to be sattvic.

10

The intelligent one
who lets go
cuts away doubt
and is filled with truth;
that one does not cling

to auspicious action,
and does not hate
inauspicious action.

11

Indeed, the one
who bears a body
is not able
to let go of actions
entirely;
the one who lets go
of the fruit of action
is called a *tyagi*.

12

For those who do not let go
when they die,
the fruit of action
exists in three kinds:
wanted, unwanted
and mixed together.
But for those who let go,
there is no fruit at all.

13

Strong-Armed One,
awaken to
these five causes
taught by me
and told in the teachings
of *samkhya*
for the fulfilment
of all actions:

14

the body as
the place of action;
the agent;

the means of different kinds;
the different motions,
each unique;
and divine will,
the fifth cause.

15
These are
the five causes
of whatever actions
one begins
with mind, word
or body,
whether customary
or contrary to custom.[2]

16
This being true,
the one who sees
his own self
as the only agent
is hard-headed,
and does not see,
because of insight
which is incomplete.

17
The one who has
no sense of 'mine'
and whose insight
is not stained,
that one is not bound
and does not kill,
even when he kills
these very people.

18

The three kinds
of impulses for action
are the wisdom of knowledge,
the knower
and that which is to be known.
The three factors of action
are the agent, the act
and the means.

19

In accounting
for the *gunas*,
it is told that wisdom
of knowledge, action and means
are also threefold,
distinguished by *gunas*.
Listen properly
to these, also.[3]

20

That wisdom of knowledge
by which one sees
the imperishable
in all beings,
and the whole
in multiplicities –
recognize that wisdom
as sattvic.

21

But that wisdom
which understands
different natures
of different kinds,
each separate

in all beings –
recognize that wisdom
as rajasic.

22

But that which clings
to only one action
to be done
without motive,
trifling
and without true aim –
that is said
to be tamasic.

23

That action
which is free from clinging
and restrained, performed
without hatred or desire,
without longing
to acquire the fruit,
that action is said
to be sattvic.

24

But that action
performed
with longing to acquire,
with a strong sense
of 'I', or further,
with much striving,
is said
to be rajasic.

25

That action begun
because of delusion,
without heeding

the consequences,
or the effects of power,
or loss, or injury,
is said
to be tamasic.

26

The actor who is free
from clinging and talk of self,
who is accompanied by
effort and courage,
unchanged by fulfilment
or lack of fulfilment,
is said
to be sattvic.

27

The passionate actor
longing to acquire
the fruit of action,
impure, greedy,
whose nature is violent
and filled with pain and pleasure,
is said
to be rajasic.

28

The actor who is
stubborn and vulgar,
not joined to *yoga*,
lazy, false and wicked,
despondent and
procrastinating,
is said
to be tamasic.

29
Arjuna,
Winner of Wealth,
now hear
the three kinds
of insight and courage,
according to the *guna*s,
set forth completely,
one by one.

30
Son of Pritha, that insight
which distinguishes
exertion from inertia;
that to be done
from that not to be done;
that to be feared
from that not to be feared,
is sattvic.

31
And, Son of Pritha,
the insight
which does not
distingish correctly
between *dharma* and its absence,
between that to be done
and that not to be done,
is rajasic.

32
Son of Pritha,
the insight
wrapped in darkness
which thinks
that all things are backwards,

and that the *dharma*
is its absence,
is tamasic.

33

Son of Pritha,
by *yoga* which does not stray,
the steadiness with which
one maintains the actions
of the senses,
the vital breath and the mind,
that steadiness
is sattvic.

34

But Arjuna, Son of Pritha,
the steadiness with which
one maintains wealth,
desire and *dharma*,
longing for the fruit
with clinging,
that steadiness
is rajasic.

35

Son of Pritha,
the steadiness with which
a dull-witted one
holds on to
pride and despondence,
or pain, fear and sleep,
that steadiness
is tamasic.

36

But now, hear from me,
Bull of the Bharatas,
the three grades of joy[4]

which one can
experience
through practice,
and arrive at an end
of sorrow:

37

that joy which is like poison
in the beginning,
and is like nectar
when transformed,
born from clarity
in the insight of the self,
is said
to be sattvic;

38

that joy which is like nectar
in the beginning,
and poison
when transformed
through contact between
the senses and their objects,
is known
as rajasic;

39

and that joy which
in its beginning
and in its end
deludes the self,
and arises from
confusion, laziness
and sleep, is said
to be tamasic.

40
There is no being
on earth,
or in heaven,
or among the gods –
no being
who is free
from these three *guna*s
born of nature.

41
Scorcher of the Enemy,
the actions
of brahmin priests,
kshatriya warriors
and *vaishya* merchants
are portioned out
by the *guna*s,
sources of each innate nature.

42
Brahmin action is born from
the nature within:
calmness, restraint,
heated discipline,
purity, patience,
honesty, wisdom,
discernment
and a sense of presence.

43
Warrior action
is born from
the nature within:
might, inner light,
courage and skill,

and not fleeing in battle,
generosity
and a lordly temperament.

44
Vaishya merchant action
is born from
the nature within:
trade, cow-herding and ploughing;
and the action of service
is born from
the nature within
of shudras, those who serve.

45
Content in
one's own action,
one gains complete fulfilment.
Hear then how
one who is
content in
his own action
finds fulfilment:

46
honouring
by one's own action
the one from whom
all beings come forth,
the one by whom
all the world is pervaded,
a human being
finds fulfilment.

47
One's own *dharma*,
however badly done,
is a higher good than

another's *dharma*,
however well done;
if one performs action
as set down by one's own nature,
one does not create fault.

48

Son of Kunti,
one should not let go
of one's natural action,
even if it is flawed.
All beginnings
are surrounded
by error, as fire
is surrounded by smoke.[5]

49

With insight
that clings to nothing,
with longing passed away,
one's self subdued,
through renunciation
one goes to
the highest fulfilment
in the state beyond action.

50

Son of Kunti,
learn from me briefly:
the one who has
found fulfilment
also gains
Brahman,
the highest state
of wisdom.

51
Joined to pure insight
and restraining the self
with steadiness,
letting go
of the objects of sense,
starting with sound,[6]
throwing aside
passion and hatred,

52
consuming lightly,
dwelling apart,
controlled in body, mind and speech,
eternally holding
the *yoga* of meditation
as the highest end,
taking refuge
in a state without passion,

53
releasing pride, force
and the focus on 'I'
of grasping,
anger and desire,
at peace and without
a sense of 'mine',
one becomes fit
for the being of Brahman.

54
The one whose self
is tranquil,
of one being with Brahman,
who neither grieves nor desires,
for whom all beings

are the same,
gains the highest
devotion to me.

55
Through devotion to me
one comes to know
how far I reach;
and who I truly am.
And then,
when one knows me truly,
one enters me
in an instant.

56
Further, if one
is always performing
all actions
while taking refuge
in me, one reaches
through my grace
an imperishable,
unchanging home.

57
Renouncing
by thought
all actions to me,
and holding me
as the highest,
take refuge
in the *yoga* of insight,
and think of me always.

58
When you think of me,
through my grace
you will cross into

all those places
so hard to reach,
but if you cannot listen,
from a sense of 'mine',
you will die.

59

If you take refuge
in the sense of 'mine',
and think,
'I will not fight',
your resolve
is hopeless,
and the force of nature
will command you.

60

Son of Kunti,
through that which arises
out of your own nature,
bound by your own action
in confusion
you will do
even that which
you do not want to do.

61

Arjuna,
the lord of all beings
dwells in the place
of the heart,
and causes all beings
to wander in illusion,
as if following
a great cosmic map.

62

Son of Bharata,
go, with your whole being,
to that one refuge,
and from that grace
you will reach
the eternal
dwelling place,
and the highest peace.

63

So this wisdom
told to you by me
is more hidden
than the hidden;
and when you have
pondered this
completely,
then do as you like.

64

Even further,
listen to
my highest word:
the most hidden of all;
you are greatly
loved by me,
so I will speak
for your benefit.[7]

65

Devoted to me,
keep your mind intent on me,
give honour to me,
and sacrifice to me.
In this way, you will

truly go to me,
I promise,
for you are my beloved.

66

Letting go
of all *dharma*s,
take me alone
as your place of rest,
and do not grieve,
because I will
free you
from all evils.

67

This should never be spoken
by you to one
who lacks the heat of discipline,
or who is not
devoted to me,
or who does not want
to hear what is to be said,
or who sneers at me.

68

The one who sets forth
this highest, hidden truth
to those who
are devoted to me,
and has shown
the highest love for me,
will without a doubt
go to me.

69

No one
among all humankind
will give

more love to me,
and there will be
no other on earth
dearer to me
than that one.

70
And my thought is this:
one who learns
and recites
this conversation of ours
so filled with *dharma*
would sacrifice to me
with the sacrifice
of knowledge.

71
And also
one who would hear
without sneering,
full of trust,
would be freed,
and would reach
those happy worlds
where actions are pure.

72
Son of Pritha,
have you listened
to this
with focused thought?
Have your ignorance
and confusion
been taken away,
Winner of Wealth?

Arjuna said:

73
Unfailing Krishna,
through your grace,
I have gained
wise memory,
and lost delusion.
I stand here
with my doubt gone.
I will do what you say.

Sanjaya said:

74
Thus, I have heard
the conversation between
the son of Vasudeva
and the son of Pritha,
whose nature is great.
It was miraculous
and caused my hair
to stand on end!

75
By the grace of Vyasa,
the composer,
I have heard
this highest,
hidden *yoga*
from Krishna, lord of *yoga*,
speaking himself,
right before my eyes.

76
King,
remembering
continually

this miraculous
and sacred dialogue
between Arjuna
and lovely-haired Krishna,
I rejoice again and again.

77

King,
remembering
again and again
the miraculous
form of Hari[8]
my wonder is great,
and I rejoice
again and again.

78

This is my thought:
wherever there is Krishna,
the lord of *yoga*,
wherever there is Arjuna,
Son of Pritha, bearing his bow,
there will always be splendour,
victory, well-being,
and wise conduct.

Glossary of Names

Agni the god of fire, also the actual fire in the Vedic sacrifice

Arjuna Pandava brother, main character of the *Gita*, known for his skill in battle

Aryaman minor sun deity in Vedic times, symbolizing hospitality, chief of the ancestors

Bhima one of the Pandava brothers of Arjuna, known for his fierceness in battle

Bhishma great-uncle of the Pandava brothers, fighting on the Kaurava side in the war

Bhrigu one of the great Vedic sages, and progenitor of a powerful early Indian family

Brihaspati god of speech, said to inspire eloquence in sacrificial performance

Cekitana warrior of the Pandavas, whose name means 'the intelligent one'

Daityas enemies of the gods; allied with the Asuras in competition with the gods

Dhrishtasaketu warrior of the Pandavas, whose name means 'the bold leader'

Dhrishthadyumna Pandava warrior, son of Drupada, whose name means 'power of strength'

Dhritarashtra blind king, father of the Kauravas (and therefore uncle of the Pandavas), and, through Sanjaya's narration, witness to the great battle

Draupadi common wife of the five Pandava brothers, known for her endurance

Drona common childhood teacher of the warrior arts of both Pandavas and Kauravas

Drupada king and ally of the Pandavas, father of Draupadi; name means 'quick step'

Duryodhana eldest of the Kaurava brothers, fiercely jealous of the Pandavas' privilege

Gandhari wife of Dhritarashtra, mother of the hundred Kaurava sons

Garuda great bird-vehicle of Vishnu, of whom Krishna is the *avatara*

Hari epithet of both Krishna and the larger deity, Vishnu

Ikshvaku great family dynasty spawning the Bharatas (Kauravas and Pandavas)

Indra warrior god of the Vedic sacrifice, with great appetites and fierceness

Janaka learned king of ancient India, both a warrior and a sage

Jayadratha a Kaurava warrior

Kandarpa name of the Hindu deity Kama, lord of desire

Karna son of Kunti and Surya, the sun god, half-brother of the Pandavas, fighting on the Kaurava side

Kripa a Kaurava warrior, chief priest at Hastinapura and brother-in-law of Drona

Krishna Vrishni prince, Arjuna's charioteer who is also *avatara* of the Hindu god Vishnu

Kunti Pandu's first wife, mother of the Pandavas, also called Pritha

Kuntibhoja foster-father of Kunti, who adopted her into the Yadava clan

Madhu (1) demon slain by Vishnu, of whom Krishna is an *avatara*; (2) ancestor of the Yadava people, Krishna's clan

Madri Pandu's second wife after Kunti, mother of the twins Nakula and Sahadeva

Manu law-giver and progenitor of the human race

Meru cosmic mountain seated at the centre of the universe

Nakula one of the two youngest Pandava brothers, twin of Sahadeva

Pandavas five sons of Pandu, enemy of the Kauravas in the *Mahabharata*

Pandu the Pale One, father of the Pandavas and husband of Kunti

Parikshit grandson of the Pandavas, survivor of a night raid by the Kauravas

Parjanya the Vedic god of rain, and, relatedly, of abundance

Prahlada Indian prince, former enemy of the gods, who moved to their side

Prajapati a creator god in early Indian texts; ordainer of rituals

Pritha epithet of Kunti, and her original name before she adopted that of her foster-father

Purujit Pandava warrior, whose name means 'conquering widely'

Rudras storm gods of the Vedic world; companions of Indra

Sahadeva one of the two youngest Pandava brothers, twin of Nakula

Sanjaya minister of the Kauravas and envoy between the two warring factions

Satyaki Pandava warrior, kinsman of Krishna, known for his skill as archer

Shaibya Pandava warrior, king of the Shibis, traditional allies of the Pandavas

Shankara ninth-century CE philosopher of non-dualism, and commentator on the *Gita*

Shikhandin Pandava warrior, who in an earlier life as a woman vowed to kill Bhishma

Somadatta Kaurava warrior, ancient competitor with Krishna's kinsmen

Subhadra Krishna's sister, daughter of Vasudeva and wife of Arjuna

Sura Pandava warrior, cousin of Kuntibhoja, Kunti's foster-father

Surya sun god, and actual sun, in the Vedic world; father of Karna

Ushanas great Vedic poet, also known as craftsman of skill

Uttamaujas Pandava warrior, whose name means 'highest power'

Vainateya name of Garuda, the great bird-vehicle of Vishnu

Vasishtha great Vedic sage, known for his protection of wealth and the home

Vasudeva father of Krishna, and, with long 'a' in 'Vasu', a patronymic of Krishna himself

Vasu a bright god, usually associated with the sun

Vasuki king of serpents

Vayu the wind god, and the actual wind, in the Vedic sacrifice

Virata Pandava warrior, king of the realm where the Pandavas live in hiding, just before the great war

Vittesha lord of wealth among the Yakshas and Rakshas, nature and guardian semi-divine beings

Vivasvat god of the sun (also known as Surya), teller of the secret of *yoga*, and father of the progenitor of humans, Manu

Vrishni western Indian clan, over whom Krishna rules; their major city was Dvaraka

Vyasa author of and witness to the *Mahabharata*; ancestor of both sides of the war

Yudhamanyu Pandava warrior, whose name means 'passionate in battle'

Yudhishthira eldest of the Pandava brothers, known for his sagacity

Yuyudhana Pandava warrior (also known as Satyaki, see above), whose name means 'wanting to fight'

Commonly Used Epithets

A first-time reader might find a list of epithets useful. Although they can be daunting at first, these epithets give richness, texture and even irony to the conversation between the two characters.

Many epithets are used as a result of the family lineage. Thus, Arjuna is frequently called a member of the Bharata clan, as well as the Son of Kunti and Son of Pandu. Arjuna is also called a descendant of the Kurus. This epithet does *not* mean he is on the Kaurava side of the war between the Pandavas and the Kauravas. Rather, it refers to the fact that Kuru, the great patriarch, was a common ancestor for both sets of cousins, and both sides of the war.

So, too, Krishna is called by his family names, such as that of the Vrishni clan or the Yadava people; he is also called Son of Vasudeva, his father. It is important to note two uses of Madhu here. Krishna is called both a Son of Madhu, from his ancestor of that name, and the Killer of Madhu, based on the name of the demon whom Vishnu destroyed. (Remember that, as the Tenth and Eleventh Discourses powerfully remind us, Krishna is an *avatara* of Vishnu.) Note that, as great warriors, *both* Arjuna and Krishna are called 'Strong-Armed One'.

EPITHETS FOR ARJUNA

Best of the Bharatas
Best of the Kurus
Blameless One
Brave Kuru
Bull among Men
Bull of the Bharatas
Joy of the Kurus
Scorcher of the Enemy
Son of Bharata
Son of Kunti
Son of Kuru
Son of Pandu
Son of Pritha
Strong-Armed One

Thick-Haired One
Tiger among Men
Winner of Wealth

EPITHETS FOR KRISHNA

Blessed One
Bristling-Haired One
Imperishable One
Killer of Keshin (a demon)
Killer of Madhu (a demon, killed by Vishnu, of whom Krishna is an *avatara*)
Killer of the Enemy
Krishna of the Yadu (one of the Yadava clan)
Mover of Men
Son of Madhu (a patriarch of the Yadava clan)
Son of Vrishni
Son of Vasudeva
Strong-Armed One

Notes

FIRST DISCOURSE

1. *said these words*: I have generally, but not exclusively, translated Sanskrit terms for 'word' as plural 'words' to connote the sense of 'an utterance', 'a speech' or 'a sentence'. To 'speak a speech' or 'speak an utterance' is awkward in English; and the singular 'word' does not suffice for the sense of a longer 'discourse' which is communicated by the text. (For an exception see verse 18.64.)
2. *Drupada's son*: Dhrishtadyumna (lit., strong courage) is the son of the King Drupada, a staunch ally of the Pandavas and chief of the Pandava army. Dhrishtadyumna is also Drona's pupil, hence the pain of fellow-students fighting each other in war.
3. *Great heroes . . . with the great chariot*: 'Yuyudhana' means 'wanting to fight', and is another name for Satyaki. Satyaki/Yuyudhana is a Vrishni kinsman of Krishna's. He fought on the Pandava side, and is known for his skill as a warrior, having once acted as Krishna's charioteer. With Krishna, he attempted the final peace agreement before the war broke out, and was involved in many infamous battles during the progress of the war. Virata is the name of the king who received the Pandava brothers in disguise during their last year in exile. While he did not recognize the Pandavas during their stay with him, he became an ally of their cause later during the start of battle. In addition to being the father of Draupadi, Drupada is a rival of Drona, instructor in the martial arts of both the Pandavas and the Kauravas at Hastinapura. Drona was a former childhood friend who was angry at Drupada for going back on a promise he had made in his youth. Drupada produced a son, Dhrishthadyumna, for the sole purpose of killing Drona in the war.
4. *Kuntibhoja*: The foster-father of Kunti, the Pandavas' mother. Kuntibhoja adopted her from his cousin Sura, also a Yadava

prince. Kunti's original name was Pritha, and she took his name, Kunti, as a way of doing honour to him. Thus, two of Arjuna's names are Partha, son of Pritha, and Kaunteya, son of Kunti.

5. *Mighty Yudhamanyu . . . with great chariots*: Subhadra was most beloved of Arjuna, and after many trials, he was finally able to make her his wife, and carried her off with Krishna's permission. Her son Abhimanyu, mentioned in this verse, was a great warrior whose loss was greatly mourned by the Pandavas. The 'Sons of Draupadi' here are the Pandavas' sons.

6. *You Drona . . . of Somadatta too*: Drona is the famed teacher of martial arts in the Hastinapura kingdom, who taught both the Kauravas and the Pandavas from childhood. Kripa was the chief priest of the court of Hastinapura, and brother-in-law of Drona, whom his twin sister married. He fought on the Kaurava side. At the end of the war he was appointed as the teacher of Parikshit, Arjuna's grandson and survivor of the war. Somadatta originally competed for the hand of Devaki, Krishna's mother, and lost to Satyaki. He thus has an ancient rivalry with Satyaki's family which was played out in the great battle of the *Mahabharata*. Somadatta's son, Bhurishravas, fought on the Kaurava side and lost his life in a vicious battle with Satyaki.

7. *is bounded*: The Sanskrit is ambiguous here. *Aparyaptam* traditionally means 'not sufficient', but this translation would not make sense, as Duryodhana would then be admitting his army is not sufficient, when his army is in fact larger than that of the Pandavas. Van Buitenen ('A Contribution to the Critical Edition of the *Bhagavadgita*', *Journal of the American Oriental Society*, 85 (Jan.–March 1965), 103) has suggested, following an earlier recension of the text, that the two names were originally transposed. This earlier recension would then mean that Duryodhana was stating that his own army (and therefore that of Bhishma) was indeed sufficient, and that of Bhima and the Pandavas was inadequate. I have decided to go with an alternative reading of *aparyaptam*, which would mean 'unbounded' or 'unlimited'. Then the verse as it is would make some sense.

8. *guarded by Bhishma . . . protect Bhishma*: There are several word-plays in verses 10 and 11. Edgerton and others have noticed that Bhishma and Bhima are contrasted in verse 10; and here, the phrases for 'guarded by Bhishma' and 'protect Bhishma' both come from the same root, *abhi√raksh*. My own sense is that this word-play also shows the ancient warrior's vulnerability as well as his strength, and is perhaps a slight hint at his coming death.

9. *The bristling-haired Krishna*: *Hrishikesha* is the term I have translated as 'bristling-haired'. The term literally means 'hair that is agitated', and tends to connote 'alert', 'aware' or 'excited'. One alternative reading is that of *hrishika* + *isha*, which would mean 'Lord over that which is agitated', i.e. 'Lord of the Senses'. (The English 'bristling-haired' does not give the sense of full awareness that the Sanskrit compound does, and yet one must live with such imperfections.)
10. *The One from Kashi . . . still unconquered*: Dhrishtadyumna is born fully grown as the son of Drupada, who performs a sacrifice for powerful offspring so that he might vanquish Drupada's rival, the teacher Drona. Shikhandin was born first as Amba, a woman rejected in marriage by the cousins' great-uncle Bhishma. She vowed to kill Bhishma because of her humiliation, and was reborn as Shikhandini, daughter of Drupada. She was raised as a boy, but when given in marriage to a woman, her sex was revealed. She then exchanged her sex with a Yaksha, and finished her life as a Pandava warrior who, with Arjuna, did indeed help to kill Bhishma.
11. *the Son of Pandu . . . raised his bow*: Arjuna's banner was decorated with sign of a monkey. Some scholars have made the comparison to Hanuman, the devotee and 'right-hand man' of Lord Rama, in Valmiki's epic the *Ramayana*, possibly composed slightly later than the *Mahabharata*.
12. *thick-haired Arjuna*: *Gudakesha* is the Sanskrit term for 'thick-haired'. It is being compared to *hrishikesha*, Krishna's 'bristling hair'. *Guda* also has the meaning of molasses of sugar cane, thus connoting sweetness as well as thickness.
13. *the son of Kunti*: In the use of the epithet *Kaunteya* here there may be an implied sense that Arjuna shares this status with both his brothers and with Karna, who fights on the other side. Thus, this epithet adds a subtler level of pathos to Arjuna's despair.
14. *my hair bristles*: This bristling would have been of a very different kind from the bristling associated with Krishna's state of constant awareness. In Arjuna's case, it is a sign of agitation.
15. *Lord of the Cows*: This epithet refers to Krishna's mythological role as a cow-herd in his youth.
16. *life-breath and wealth*: The suggestion here is that both sides, Kauravas and Pandavas, have shared the same ambitions, dreams and desires in childhood and adolescence.
17. *Killer of Madhu*: There is, I think, some irony in the use of this epithet for Krishna here in this particular verse. Krishna is known for slaying the demon Madhu – one of his great feats. In this

discussion of killing and death, Arjuna is referring to the fact that Krishna too is a killer – but of demons, not relatives.

18. *Son of Madhu*: Arjuna is referring not to the demon Madhu, mentioned in verse 35, but Krishna's ancestor Madhu, who gave birth to the Yadava race, Krishna's people. Again it seems appropriate, in a verse discussing his own kinsmen, for Arjuna to use this epithet for Krishna in an implied contrast to the earlier reference and a means of transmitting caste rules.

19. *Son of Vrishni*: In his earthly form, Krishna is a member of the Vrishni clan, or tribe, that hails from west of the Hastinapura kingdom.

20. ... *the corruption of women*: This verse might be hard for a twenty-first-century reader to understand. The idea is, in part, that women are particular bearers of virtue, and if they are corrupted, duties according to caste, or social role, are also corrupted. The reader might want to consult *The Laws of Manu*, 3.55–6 and 9.2–31 for more discussion of this issue.

21. *offerings of rice and water*: In early India, as well as in some parts of Hindu India today, traditional offerings of rice balls and water (*pinda*) would be offered to the ancestors as homage and food. Such offerings would keep them in their lofty stations as honoured ancestors in the next world. The ancestors 'fell' or were consigned to hell if not fed properly.

22. ... *a blending of caste*: There is an intriguing parallel here being made between the avoidance of *dharma* and the mixing of caste. Arjuna is speaking about one kind of destruction of family in war, and Krishna is speaking about another kind, through the mixture of caste roles.

SECOND DISCOURSE

1. *a noble one*: The term that is used here is *arya*. *Arya* in early Sanskrit means a righteous, well spoken and high-born person. Obviously the term connotes something rather different in its earliest Sanskrit meaning than 'Aryan' does today, after its appropriation by the Nazis and later groups.

2. *a cowardly eunuch*: Sanskrit *klaibyam* has the sense of both 'a eunuch' or emasculated person, and a coward.

3. *Scorcher of the Enemy*: This epithet might well be used by Krishna as a form of encouraging Arjuna, referring as it does to his prowess in war.

4. *Better to eat . . . lordship of the gods*: Verses 5–8 are composed in *trishtubh* metre, which is a frequent alternative metre to that of the *shloka* in the epic. It consists of eleven syllables rather than the eight of the usual *shloka* metre. Some have argued that the metrical switch is due to emotional content.
5. *Scorcher of the Enemy*: Here, Sanjaya is speaking to Dhritarashtra again, describing the battle, and we return briefly to the first 'frame' of the *Gita*.
6. *the embodied self*: *Dehin*. The term is also reminiscent of the teaching of the Upanishads, which first introduce the idea of *atman*, a self (some translate 'soul') independent of the body and which moves through cycles of transmigration, or *samsara*. *Dehin*, literally 'the embodied one', is used frequently in the *Gita*. See *Brihadaranyaka Upanishad* 6.2.15–16, *Chandogya Upanishad* 4.15.5–6 and 5.10.1–8 and *Kaushitaki Upanishad* 1.2–5.
7. *son of Bharata*: Here, in contrast to verse 10, Krishna is referring to Arjuna, not Dhritarashtra, as a descendant of Bharata. Both Arjuna and his uncle Dhritarashtra are, of course, descendants of their great ancestor Bharata.
8. *Unborn*: In a world-view which includes the transmigration of the self from birth to death and death to birth, to be 'unborn' would mean that one's real nature is ultimately unaffected by *samsara*, or has the capacity to transcend it. That is the liberated state known as *moksha*. Both the self and Krishna are described as 'unborn' in the *Gita* (see 2.21, 4.6, 7.25 and 10.12).
9. *The self is not born . . . when the body is killed*: This verse switches to *trishtubh* metre. The same applies to verses 22, 29 and 30.
10. *Strong-Armed One*: Krishna may be using this epithet as a way of referring to Arjuna's strength, and shoring him up in his grief.
11. *this insight . . . the bonds of action*: Krishna is most likely explaining here that *samkhya* is a form of knowledge and that *yoga*, in the usage of this verse, is the *yoga* of action. Krishna also occasionally refers to *samkhya* as the '*yoga* of knowledge', so it is important to be clear.
12. *Veda*: The word means 'knowledge'. The four Vedas were collections of poetic formulae, or mantras, that accompanied the sacrifice – a vegetable or animal offering to the gods. In verses 42–5, Krishna may well be referring to Vedic practices and schools of thoughts, such as Mimamsa, where desire for heaven was understood as a legitimate goal.
13. *free of the three gunas, free from opposites*: *Guna*s are the three qualities pervading the universe. Here Krishna is subsuming the

Vedas, which were originally thought to be the totality of knowledge, into the larger scheme of *samkhya*, which also purports to account for everything in the universe.

14. *Your authority ... to inaction*: Here, Krishna is beginning to make an argument for the *yoga* of action. Neither action, nor inaction, neither being-in-the-world, nor renunciation, has merit if it is done with a clinging attitude and an attachment to the results. Each action is done with moral grounding of *dharma*, and all must be done, as verse 49 states, with insight (*buddhi*).

15. *and may be heard [again]*: Here Krishna is referring to *shruti*, or 'that which is heard'. *Shruti* usually includes the four Vedas and their branches, and is understood as passed down orally, from generation to generation. It is distinct from *smriti*, 'that which is remembered'. The epics are usually understood as *smriti*, but many classify the *Mahabharata* as a 'fifth Veda', implying that its powers are as revelatory as the Vedas.

16. *... the highest*: Taste was understood to be the deepest of the five senses. This verse refers to one who has abstained from food. The 'highest' here might well be Brahman, or it may refer to Krishna himself.

17. *who knows the tremor of reality*: The Sanskrit word *vipascitah* is usually translated as 'wise ones'. I have translated it more concretely as 'who knows the tremor of reality'. The term comes from the root *vip*, 'to shake'. The compound is *vipa*s + *cit* – 'those who see or know vibrations' or 'those who see or know trembling'. The various verbs in this verse strike one forcibly as playing on all the senses of struggle that such yogic discipline involves.

18. *concentrate*: The idea here is an expansion of focus; the Sanskrit term *bhavana* implies an experience, or being, of the mind.

19. *The restrained one ... who sees*: This verse and the next contain reversals of what one traditionally expects – confirming the idea that yogic discipline is a counter-intuitive process. In the reverse imagery of day and night, Krishna is arguing that the sage's states of awareness are the reverse of those who are not engaged by *yoga*. In the imagery of the ocean (verse 70), Krishna is reversing our awareness of the constantly moving ocean, and reminding us that it has a core stability and grounding.

20. *As the ocean ... desires desire*: This verse contains an extraordinary insight, reminiscent of the theory of René Girard that desire's real object is not another object, such as a person, or a food, or a possession. Rather, its object is desire itself. One wants another's desiring. Krishna implies here that, for one who is

attached, desire multiplies itself and becomes its own object. One desires a life of desire, flitting from object to object.

21. *The person . . . that one comes to peace*: Although I have chosen to interpret most masculine pronouns in the text as 'generic masculines' which could theoretically be open to both genders, here the language is indeed masculine. The Sanskrit term *pumsa* is used to denote that person who can attain peace; in that period, of course, the tendency was for that person capable of attaining peace to be male. For the sake of clarity and consistency I chose to translate 'person'.

22. *the bliss of cessation*: Brahman is used here as a state of being, a state caused by refuge in Krishna himself. The term *nirvana* is not used in the Buddhist sense, but in a more general sense. Cessation does not imply, as the Buddhist would argue, a 'non-self', but rather a cessation of desire (see also verses 5.24–6 and 6.15). The use of the term here has suggested to many scholars, however, that the *Gita* was composed when early followers of the Buddha and other ascetic groups were debating these very issues.

THIRD DISCOURSE

1. *such terrible action*: *Ghora* has the double sense of 'terrible' and 'sublime'.

2. *the yoga of knowledge . . . who practise yoga*: Krishna is again distinguishing between the *yoga* of action (*karma*) and the *yoga* of knowledge (*jñana*, found in the school of *samkhya*), as he did previously in verse 2.39, and will do in many other moments in the *Gita*.

3. *beyond action*: *Naishkarmya* here is the state of not needing to act, the state beyond action. It is slightly distinguished from 'non-action' per se. We recall verse 2.47, where Krishna first began this discussion of the relationship between action and non-action.

4. *As you both . . . the higher good*: The idea of 'mutual self-creation' is a common one in early Indian texts. One might note the Vedic 'from the man came Viraj, and from Viraj came the man', where the feminine and masculine principles create each other in *Rig Veda* 10.129.5.

5. *The true ones . . . only for themselves*: Here again, Krishna is employing traditional sacrificial imagery and challenging the

presumed views. For Krishna, those who eat the leftovers are those who are purer, whereas those who eat only what they have cooked in their own sacrificial interests are less pure. Even within the realm of sacrificial action, one can act without regard to the fruits. This verse, as well as the two following it, addresses the larger question of sacrificial action as a model for all action. Commentators differ as to whether just sacrificial action or all action is meant. What is clear is that a relationship between the two is being established.

6. *Beings exist . . . exists through action*: This idea of the cycle, whereby sacrifice produces rain (Parjanya, the Vedic god of rain), and rain produces food, and food produces creatures, is a common one in the early Indian world. See, for example, *Taittiriya Upanishad* 2.3.

7. *the eternal nature*: *Aksharam*, which I here translate as 'eternal nature', could also mean the eternal syllable 'Om'. This idea of an eternal syllable is a frequent image beginning as early as the *Rig Veda*.

8. *gained fulfilment*: *Samsiddhi* (and other words relating to *siddha*) is translated here as 'fulfilment'. It is often translated as 'perfection' or 'success', but the sense of joy and completion implied by the word 'fulfilment' means more to a twenty-first-century readership than the worldly, goal-oriented language of achievement connoted by the words 'perfection' and 'success'. Janaka was reputed to be an ancient king of Mithila, and equal in wisdom as in bravery. He was the pupil of the great sage Yajñavalkya in the Upanishads, and thus knew the meaning of *atman*, or the self, in addition to his acts of bravery. Janaka is also the father of the heroine Sita in the epic the *Ramayana*. In this verse he is modelled as the ideal enlightened actor in the world.

9. *to keep the world collected together*: This idea of 'maintenance of the world' (*lokasamgraha*) was one of the ideas that M. K. Gandhi held dear. By observing disciplined, equanimous actions, with a view towards Krishna, one literally holds the world together in both a spiritual and material sense.

10. *a fire which is always hungry*: Most forms of early Indian thought, whether Buddhist, Brahmanical or Jain, understood desire as a form of fire.

FOURTH DISCOURSE

1. *I create myself*: Krishna may be referring to the idea of the *avatara* – literally, the 'crossing down' of a god to earth in order to right a wrong or redress an imbalance. Vishnu, of whom Krishna is an *avatara*, is known for his many life-saving *avatara*s on earth.
2. *The four castes . . . who does not act*: The four *varna*s, or castes, are also involved in the working of the *guna*s. Commentators up through the present century have argued vociferously about whether the *Gita* is a proponent of discrimination according to caste or against it. Depending on which verses one emphasizes, both views can be supported.
3. *Action was taken . . . who sought freedom*: Krishna is explaining that *moksha*, or release from the cycle of transmigration, was possible for those who undertook action with insight; *moksha* was not simply the domain of those who renounced action.
4. *Brahman is offering . . . the action of Brahman*: One is reminded here of a passage in J. D. Salinger's 'Teddy' (1954): '"I was six when I saw that everything was God, and my hair stood up, and all," Teddy said. "It was on a Sunday, I remember. My sister was a tiny child then, and she was drinking her milk, and all of a sudden I saw that she was God and the milk was God. I mean, all she was doing was pouring God into God, if you know what I mean."' Salinger had read the work of the Hindu saint Ramakrishna.
5. *Some who practise yoga . . . the fire of Brahman*: This verse is probably a reference to *Rig Veda* 10.129.5, which ends with the gods sacrificing to the sacrifice with the sacrifice. Yet unlike *Rig Veda* 10.129.5, Brahman is the all-encompassing principle here. Throughout these next few verses, Krishna is deliberately using the language of sacrifice to describe meditative and yogic activity.
6. *you will see all beings . . . and then in me*: The all-encompassing view of Krishna, beyond even Brahman itself, foreshadows the Tenth and Eleventh Discourses, when Krishna reveals himself fully to Arjuna, as well as the opening verses of the Twelfth Discourse.
7. *Even if you are . . . the boat of wisdom*: This verse expresses the common early Indian idea of a 'boat' or 'raft' as a tool of gradual insight. The raft is something we can become attached to but then leave behind as we attain a higher state.

FIFTH DISCOURSE

1. *Tell this to me once and for all*: Here, as in any normal conversation between teacher and pupil, Arjuna is expressing frustration that Krishna is not taking a stand between action and non-action. In verse 2, Krishna takes a stand (as the reader would now expect) in the middle, for 'non-clinging' action.
2. *the city of nine gates*: The 'city' here is the body, and the nine gates are the nine orifices of the body.
3. *his own nature*: *Svabhava* here has the sense of 'the inherent nature of things', or 'basic existence in its basic nature'. Neither has the poetic resonance of the simple word 'nature'.
4. *a dog-cooker*: *Svapaka*, an outcaste in early Indian thought, identified with a *candala*, a common term for outcaste. *The Laws of Manu* (10.51–6) defines a dog-cooker as the offspring of a *kshatriya* father and a mixed-caste mother, but other texts define a dog-cooker as a product of a low-caste, or *shudra*, father and a higher caste, usually brahmin mother. 'Cooking a dog' is also something done in an emergency, such as the time of famine, and is an extreme act. The idea here is that these opposites, such as a brahmin and a dog-cooker, are the same to the practitioner of *yoga*.
5. *cessation*: Here again, *nirvana* ('cessation') is used in the idea of the blowing out of desire. There may be a play on ideas about light here, for the one who has the light of Brahman within is also the one who blows out the flame of the fire.
6. *focusing the eye between the eyebrows*: In early Indian thought, the idea of restraint of the mind is frequently accompanied by the idea of control of the breath. Frequently this was done by concentrating on the space between the two eyebrows. Verse 8.10 mentions this practice also. It is important to understand that breath control is the beginning of meditation; its end is nothing less than *moksha*, or liberation. Even within the *Gita*, such a state is conceived of variously as being at one with Brahman, or with *purusha*, the highest spirit, or ultimately, as the end of the *Gita* states, with Krishna.

SIXTH DISCOURSE

1. *Always joining . . . with me*: In this complex verse, Krishna understands the restraint of the mind (*niyatamanasah*) as one of the basics of meditation, but also one of the basics of action. Even more, such restraint is a path to God.
2. *When one has . . . of the senses*: As in verse 15 of this same Discourse, the mind is mentioned as an organ of restraint. In *samkhya* philosophy, the mind is understood as one of the senses. Only here, the mind not only restrains itself, but also restrains the senses (*indriya*).
3. *passion*: The word I have translated here as 'by not engaging passion' (*vairagyena*) also has the sense of equanimity or indifference. It can also mean something stronger, such as aversion.
4. *skilful ways*: *Upaya*, used to describe teaching a discipline in precisely the way that the student needs, a way that is unique to his or her particular psyche. It was a common term in early Buddhist usage as well.

SEVENTH DISCOURSE

1. *only some truly know me*: Krishna is making a very strong statement here. Among even the most spiritually successful people, only a few actually know him in the entirety of his being.
2. *My material nature*: The term here is *prakriti*, discussed in the Introduction as the material nature, classified as feminine, that makes up the universe according to *samkhya* philosophy. *Prakriti* is what possesses *guna*s, or qualities, and is enlivened by *purusha*, the animating spirit.
3. *Understand . . . of the whole world*: Here, Krishna begins to reveal himself and his divine nature with a series of 'I' statements. This self-revelation will become more extensive in following Discourses, especially the Ninth, Tenth and Eleventh.
4. *the sacred syllable 'Om'*: The sacred, primordial syllable consists of three letters, *a* + *u* + *m*.
5. *desire*: In the *Gita* generally this can be understood as a form of attachment, or clinging. In this verse, however, desire for higher states, where one is free from clinging, is understood as a significant means along the path. This notion is reflected in other early Indian texts as well.

6. *Vasudeva*: Within the *Mahabharata*, Krishna is known as the son of Vasudeva, the chief of the Yadava people, and his wife Devaki. Hence Krishna is here called by a derivative of his father's name, with the first vowel in 'Vasu' lengthened.
7. *But I do not shine for all . . . and imperishable*: Krishna here is speaking of the ways in which his 'creative power' (called *maya*) contributes to the manifest world. *Maya* here is an important term for later philosophers of the school of Advaita Vedanta. They understand the term not only in its early meaning of creative power, but also in its later meaning of 'perceptive illusion'.

EIGHTH DISCOURSE

1. *at the time of departure*: Arjuna is speaking of the time of death; the sense of the verb *pra* √*ya* is 'motion forwards', 'departure'.
2. *'sending forth'*: *Visarga* has the force of 'creative power'; in early Indian cosmogonic narratives, the one who 'sends forth' in the fashioning of the cosmos is the one who wields the creative power.
3. *highest divine spirit*: *Purusha*, the *samkhya* term for the force which animates *prakriti*, or material nature. There are numerous *purushas* who animate individual conglomerates of material nature, but the highest one reigns supreme over all. For some thinkers, it is equivalent to Brahman of the Upanishads. For others, it is distinct.
4. *One should meditate . . . beyond the dark*: The *trishtubh* metre occurs in this verse and continues to verse 11. It occurs again in verse 28.
5. *a day of Brahma . . . the day and the night*: A single cycle of *yugas*, or ages, consists of four ages: the Krita, the Treta, the Dvapara and the Kali. The *yugas* are marked by increasing decay, with the first, the Krita, being the most virtuous and easiest to live in. As the *yugas* progress, the ages increase in confusion, wrongdoing and disorganization. We all exist in the Kali age, where civilization is at its worst. A cycle of *yugas* has been calculated at 4,320,000 years. A day in the life of Brahma is a common motif in many classical Hindu texts. Brahma is understood as a creator god, a personified version of Brahman. A single day in Brahma's life is a thousand *yugas*, which means the phrase frequently stands for unfathomable aeons.
6. *In light . . . one comes back again*: Verses 24–6 express the idea

of transmigration of the self – the endless cycle of death and birth to which the self is subject as long as it clings to objects. This is also known as *samsara*. The earliest idea of this is found in the Upanishads (*Chandogya Upanishad* 4.1.5.5 and 5.9.1–15 and *Brihadaranyaka Upanishad* 6.2.15–16). In the *Brihadaranyaka Upanishad*, the distinction between those who go on the 'bright moonlit path' and those who go on 'the moon-dark path' is between those who meditate and those who simply conduct rituals. The first do not return; the second return to *samsara*. Here, those who go on either path could be meditating yogins (practitioners of *yoga*), but those who know Brahman and follow the bright path do not return.

NINTH DISCOURSE

1. *a shape which is formless*: The language here (*avyakta murtina*) creates a lovely paradox. *Avyakta* connotes something which is 'unmanifest' and *murti* has the meaning of an 'image', 'aspect' or 'solidification' of something. This small paradox sets up the paradox of the next verse, one of the most profound theological paradoxes expressed in many religions. God is the generator of all things in the universe, but is not affected by them.
2. *one sitting apart*: Compare verse 4; God performs the action of sitting but does not sit with other beings. This phrase is usually understood as 'indifferent', but a concrete meaning is important.
3. *I am the intention . . . I am the poured oblation*: Here Krishna picks up with more intensity the self-disclosure begun in 7.6. 'Heated butter', *ghee*, or clarified butter, was used in the sacrifice as the primary offering into the fire. Translation as 'clarified butter' makes the text unnecessarily pedantic; 'heated butter' was my compromise between accuracy and flow.
4. *the Rig, the Sama and the Yajur Veda*: These are three of the four Vedas mentioned in the Second Discourse. The *Rig Veda* is the knowledge of the verses, the *Sama Veda* the knowledge of the chants, the *Yajur Veda* the knowledge of the ritual procedures. They are understood by some schools of thought to be the eternal sum and totality of all knowledge. The final Veda, the *Atharva Veda*, is absent. It is known to be more a manual for everyday life, and is frequently referred to as the Veda of women and *shudra*s.
5. *Those who know the Vedas . . . in heaven*: *Trishtubh* metre begins here and continues through verse 21. Soma is a sacred

drink used in the sacrifice, thought to increase eloquence and to be the source of inspiration. An entire book of the *Rig Veda* is devoted to its powers. The world of Indra, the powerful warrior god and hero of many Vedic exploits, is said to be a great heaven in which his palace is situated.

6. *heated discipline*: *Tapas* connotes a kind of ascetic meditation that many ancient sages performed. Some argue that the practice of *tapas* happens as early as the Vedic sacrifice; it certainly emerged during the Upanishadic period when meditation was becoming more pronounced. The word also implies the production of heat through intensity.
7. *vaishyas*: The third social class in ancient India, made up of merchants and agriculturalists. These workers created the wealth of the early Indian societies.
8. *shudras*: The lowest class of people in ancient India, the servants who performed manual labour and whose world was considered less pure than that of the other classes. Even in their low status, they were nonetheless considered an essential part of society.

TENTH DISCOURSE

1. *the seven great sages*: The sages were present at the creation of the world, and many texts understand them to be the first sacrificers. There are usually seven. The most common list is Kashyapa, Atri, Vasishtha, Vishvamitra, Gotama, Jamadagni and Bharadvaja. They are frequently in conversation with, and at times competition with, the gods. The Manu referred to in this verse is the progenitor of human mortals. Several Manus are named in the ancient narratives.
2. *Narada, and also Asita Devala*: Two of the composers of hymns in the *Rig Veda*, the Veda of poetic verses.
3. *Yogin*: Elsewhere in the text I have translated this as 'practitioner of *yoga*' or 'one who practises *yoga*', depending upon syllabic count. As it is awkward to use either of these two English phrases in the vocative, 'yogin' is retained here.
4. *Among the Adityas . . . the rabbit-marked moon*: The Adityas are powerful Vedic gods, offspring of the sun. Vishnu is one of their foremost, and plays a powerful role as one of the three main male deities in later classical Hinduism. Krishna is an *avatara*, or manifestation, of Vishnu. The Maruts are storm gods, and protectors of Indra, the Vedic warrior god; they move about in

a group, Marici foremost among them. In India, the craters on the moon are said to be in the shape of a rabbit, just as some Western cultures speak of the man in the moon.

5. *Among the Vedas . . . I am thought*: The *Sama Veda* is the Veda of chants, which, if not performed correctly, make the sacrifice lose its power. Indra, mentioned earlier in the *Gita*, is a warrior god with great prowess who defeated the demon Vritra, and gave water to the world.

6. *Among the Rudras . . . I am Meru*: Rudras are the Vedic gods who 'roar'. Shankara is said to be the foremost among them, and the antecedent of the classical god Shiva. Yakshas are semi-divine beings who dwell in the forest and guard thresholds. Rakshas are protectors, but in the main are known as demonic figures who compete with the gods for the goods of the sacrifice. Vittesha is also better known as Kubera, the lord of wealth and earthly abundance. Vasus are bright gods, frequently associated with the sun, as is fire. Meru is the cosmic mountain said to exist at the centre of the universe, sustaining it and balancing it.

7. *Skanda*: In classical Hindu mythology, Skanda is the god Shiva's son, and is independently known as a god of war.

8. *I am Bhrigu . . . soft recitation*: Bhrigu was considered the most illustrious of sages, who rivalled the gods and to whom they came for advice. The softly recited sacrifice is called *japa*, and it is frequently translated as 'muttering', which does not do justice to the idea behind this kind of recitation.

9. *Among all the trees . . . Kapila*: The *ashvattha* tree is a sacred tree used in the sacrifice and has other powerful, transformative properties. Narada is, as mentioned previously, a composer of Vedic hymns and was a well-known sage. The Gandharvas are celestial musicians whose chief is Citraratha. Kapila is said to have founded *samkhya*, the subject of so much of the *Gita*.

10. *I am Indra's Uccaihshravas . . . I am Indra's Airavata*: Indra's horse's name means 'high sounding one'. He is also the horse of Surya, the sun god. As the Hindu myth narrates, in the midst of a war with the demons, the gods agreed to churn the ocean and find the treasures hidden there, one of which was the nectar of immortality, from which Uccaihshravas emerged. Airavata is the elephant that comes from the Iravati river.

11. *I am Kandarpa . . . Vasuki*: Kandarpa is more commonly known as the god Kama, god of romantic love and sexual desire. Vasuki is the great king of serpents who traffics with the gods as well as the seers.

12. *I am Varuna . . . I am Yama, god of death*: In addition to being associated with the sea, Varuna is also a judge of sorts in the Vedas. He is the one to whom the sage Vasishtha appeals for mercy. Aryaman is a minor Vedic sun-deity, whose name means 'companion'. He is one of the Adityas, or sons of the goddess Aditi, associated with solar power. He is said to be the chief of the ancestors, to whom food offerings were given in Vedic times. Yama is the king of the underworld and in the early Vedic period the god to whom one prayed at a funeral for the safekeeping of the body.
13. *Among the Daityas . . . I am Vainateya*: A Daitya is an enemy of the gods. Prince Prahlada moved away from the side of the enemy and became a worshipper of the gods. Vainateya is more commonly known as Garuda, the splendidly colourful and energetic bird-vehicle of Vishnu – the god of whom Krishna is an *avatara*.
14. *I am Rama . . . I am Ganges, Jahnu's daughter*: Rama is the hero of the great epic, the *Ramayana*, composed slightly later than the *Mahabharata*. Rama is also an *avatara* of Vishnu. Makara can be a shark or a dolphin as well as a crocodile. Although Varuna is rarely depicted in image form, Makara is also Varuna's vehicle. Jahnu is a sage who swallowed the river Ganges. Later, after being beseeched, he let the river flow again from his ear.
15. *I am the letter 'A' . . . simple link*: 'A' is the first letter of the Sanskrit alphabet and first vowel in 'Om', the sacred syllable. The 'simple link' is a grammatical reference to the practice of joining words together in compounds (called *samasa* in Sanskrit). The simplest form of a compound is a *dvandva*, or 'two-fold' combination. It is usually a pairing, such as 'being and time' or 'boy and girl', although it may be a list of a number of related items.
16. *Among female deities . . . Endurance*: Many abstract deities in early India are feminine. These include even Ida, the sacrificial offering itself.
17. *Among chants . . . I am blossoming spring*: The great chant to Indra is named in the *Sama Veda* as one of the more auspicious chants. The Gayatri metre is a three-line metre of eight syllables each, often associated with purity. The Gayatri mantra is *Rig Veda* 3.21, and is one of the few Rig Vedic verses still recited today as part of daily worship. Margashirsha is the month of November/December, when the moon enters the fifth lunar mansion. The season of spring is neither hot nor rainy, with a

profusion of flowers and birdsong. It is pleasantly cool without the heavy rains of monsoon.

18. *Among the Vrishni people . . . the poet Ushanas*: Historically, Krishna was the son of Vasudeva, a king of the Vrishni people, to the west of the Pandava kingdom. Vyasa was a mythical sage and author of the entire *Mahabharata*. He is also grandfather to the Pandavas, and survived to tell the tale. Ushanas is the name of an ancient and powerful Vedic sage and poet.

19. *rulers with the sceptre*: The Sanskrit word *danda* refers to a rod or stick of authority, used by rulers in ancient India and metonymically extended to mean the authority of the ruler, much like 'sceptre' in current English usage.

ELEVENTH DISCOURSE

1. *See the Adityas . . . the Maruts*: For the Adityas, see n. 4 to the Tenth Discourse; for the Vasus and Rudras, see n. 6 to the Tenth Discourse; for the Maruts, see n. 4 to the Tenth Discourse. The Ashvins are twin deities, Vedic healers who travel the sky by horse and herald the dawn. All the deities have their own mode of being, which is linked to the power of their names.

2. *the divine eye*: The power to see deities in their truest form, as well as into past and future lives.

3. *If a thousand suns . . . the brilliance of that great self*: This verse was cited by Robert Oppenheimer (who knew some Sanskrit), when he witnessed the first nuclear explosion at Los Alamos.

4. *I see the gods . . . divine serpents*: The *trishtubh* metre begins again here and continues to verse 50. Much of the great manifestation of Krishna, as described by Arjuna, is thus 'marked off' by a different metre.

5. *crown, club and discus*: The traditional weapons of Vishnu, of whom Krishna is an *avatara*. They are each related to one of the functions he performs on earth.

6. *They all see you . . . those who are fulfilled*: The Sadhyas are celestial deities who dwell in the atmosphere. The 'Drinkers of Steam' (*ushmapas*) are a class of ancestors who drink the hot steam of rice balls offered in the sacrifice. For the Gandharvas, see n. 9 to the Tenth Discourse, and for the Yakshas see n. 6 to the Tenth Discourse.

7. *my self trembles . . . calm*: Here too Arjuna trembles (*pravyathita*) at the sight of Krishna. It is a sign of both agitation and awe. To

tremble is also a sign of wisdom. The text seems to be suggesting that Arjuna's fear is also a source of wisdom.

8. *As moths*: A moth is literally *patam-ga* – the flying-goer, or 'the one who goes flying'.

9. *Vishnu . . . with light*: Here, Arjuna addresses Krishna in his larger, more cosmic form of Vishnu.

10. *You are Vayu, Yama*: Vayu is the Vedic god of wind; for Yama, see n. 12 to the Tenth Discourse.

TWELFTH DISCOURSE

1. . . . *they honour me*: Verses 12.1–6 are an early expression of a centuries-old debate in India: whether the worship of god *with form* or god *without form* is a superior path. Krishna answers that both are effective ways to attain union with him.

2. . . . *that one is dear to me*: From this verse to the end of the book, Krishna focuses on the *yoga* of *bhakti*, the teaching that devotion can be a path to God as powerful as the path of *karma* or *jñana*. Although mentioned early on in the *Gita*, this idea is fully developed after the wondrous manifestation of Krishna that Arjuna experiences in the Eleventh Discourse. The Sanskrit root √*bhaj*, from which many words related to devotion are derived, is a very important and complex word with many meanings. It can mean 'to become a part of', in the sense of partial or complete union. It can also mean 'to enjoy', 'to honour', 'to devote oneself to'. But to become a part of one thing implies at times that one might be divided off from another – sometimes from one's family, sometimes from the larger world.

THIRTEENTH DISCOURSE

1. *Lovely-Haired One . . . the object of wisdom*: This verse does not occur in all versions of the text and remains unnumbered. I have translated *kshetra* and *kshetrajña* as 'sacred ground' and 'knower of sacred ground'. They are common terms in early Indian thought, and are commonly translated as 'field'. While I wanted to keep the concrete sensibility here, I also wanted to distinguish it from the very basic *kshiti*, which does mean an actual field. *Kshetra* tends to mean 'an object' and it can mean an object of desire, of thought or of knowledge. The word *kshetra*

also tends to denote the body as an object of knowledge, and all of its associated sense organs and capacities for somatic, mental and emotional experience. In this case, Arjuna is asking about *jñana*, or knowledge, and is setting up a dialogue about *samkhya* philosophy. Thus, 'sacred ground' seemed to me to get at both ideas: that of the body as a sacred object of knowledge as well as the connotation of field itself. I am grateful to Nadine Berardi for conversation about this issue.

Also in this verse, for reasons of English sense, I translate *prakriti* as 'matter' rather than 'material nature', as I do in previous verses, such as 7.4, 9.8 and 9.10.

2. *Son of Kunti . . . of the sacred ground*: Note the complexity implied in this verse. The body is the site of all knowing, even though that body is the very thing that is transcended in both *yoga* and *samkhya* philosophy. Here is an important rejoinder to the idea that *yoga* is only a body-negating discipline. On the contrary, the senses, and knowledge of the senses and their objects, are crucial to higher knowledge. One cannot ignore them; instead, one moves through them.
3. *thread-like verses*: The Sanskrit *sutra*. *Sutra* literally means 'thread', but has the larger (and less poetic) meaning of 'aphorism'. While *Brahma Sutra* is the name of a text composed later than the *Gita*, here it probably means aphorisms about Brahman.
4. *The gross elements . . . where the senses act*: The elements are ether, air, fire, water and earth. The eleven 'powers' of sense are eye, ear, skin, tongue, nose, hand, foot, mouth, anus and genitals; the eleventh is the mind. The five 'arenas' where the senses act are what in English would be called 'organs' of sense: sound, touch, sight, taste and smell.
5. *This has . . . all*: 'This' and 'It' in verses 13–17 are the *atman*, or self, as connected in its essence to Brahman.
6. *'Matter'*: At the beginning of this Discourse, the principles of *samkhya* were explained. As mentioned in n. 2 to the Seventh Discourse, *prakriti* is matter, and understood to be feminine or subordinate to *purusha*, the agent who animates all. In the Seventh Discourse *prakriti* was translated as 'material nature' when Krishna was speaking about his own nature and creation of the world. Here, it is translated as 'matter', as distinct from 'spirit', as this is the best and clearest contrast in English. Together *purusha* and *prakriti* create experiences. When they are separated from each other, *prakriti* is inert and *purusha* is unconnected spirit.

7. *Spirit abides . . . being and non-being*: When *purusha* and *prakriti* combine together in a certain form of existence, they do so based on the *gunas*, or qualities, of previous existences. Each existence's *gunas* determines how a being will be reborn into *samsara* (the endless cycle of birth, death and rebirth).
8. *The highest spirit . . . and who observes*: As it animates, the *purusha* inspires the body. Here, it is understood as the *atman*, or self, of the body. It is lord over the body and has the capacity to observe it. Many argue that this idea of 'observing power' is the best definition of *atman*.
9. *the yoga of samkhya . . . the yoga of action*: Krishna made this comparison in earlier Discourses (2.39 and 3.3).
10. *revelation*: *Shruti*, 'that which is heard' (see n. 15 to the Second Discourse). Notice here that the way of *bhakti* is acknowledged right after the other two paths (knowledge and action) are discussed.
11. *recognize . . . who knows the sacred ground*: Here, it is probable that the 'sacred ground' is *prakriti*, or material nature, and 'the one who knows' is *purusha*, or spirit.
12. *Seeing the same lord . . . the highest way*: This subtle verse shows that while the self is capable of moving beyond its clinging entanglements, the self is also capable of harming itself.
13. *Just as space . . . is not stained*: See 9.4–9.5, where a related idea is discussed. In this verse, the self abides in the body without being stained, and stands somewhat apart. So too in 9.4–9.5, all beings dwell in Krishna, but Krishna does not dwell in them. He stands apart and causes them to be.
14. *as a single sun . . . sacred ground*: The 'one who dwells in the sacred ground' is probably the self that illuminates the body.

FOURTEENTH DISCOURSE

1. *the great Brahman is my womb . . . all beings*: Here the *Gita* uses the ancient imagery of the 'womb' or 'egg' as the source of all creation. This idea is parallel to the *hiranya garbha*, or golden embryo, that gave birth to the entire world. See *Rig Veda* 10.121 for the earliest use of this image.
2. *Brahman is the great womb . . . the seeds*: The male and female imagery involved in creation here is intriguing and significant. Brahman here is styled as female. The womb, in many accounts, is styled as male.

3. *sattva . . . within the body*: As in the first verses of the Twelfth Discourse Krishna explained the relationship between *purusha* and *prakriti*, he now goes on to specify the *gunas*, or qualities, and how each of the three *gunas* creates a different kind of clinging. It is important to note here that clinging to *sattva*, the *guna* of truth, light and purity, is a vehicle to help develop a state where clinging is transcended.
4. *in the wombs of the deluded*: Wombs are not always positive images in early Indian thought. While Brahman can be understood as a 'womb' (cf. verse 4), wombs are also the means of sustaining *samsara* and hence can be a polluting space.
5. *sitting apart*: See 9.9 for a similar formulation.
6. *And the one . . . with Brahman*: Here again, *bhakti*, or devotion, is included in the ways of transcending the *gunas*.

FIFTEENTH DISCOURSE

1. *They say . . . in the Veda*: See n. 9 to the Tenth Discourse. In the Upanishads, the *ashvattha* tree is described in 'reverse', where its branches are in the ground and its roots in the air. The *ashvattha* has a lot in common with the banyan tree, where roots can grow both in the earth and in the air. The tree can be a metaphor for something which is both involved and transcendent. The metres are the sacred metres of the Veda, which give structure and significance to all the mantras chanted in the sacrifice. In later Vedic mythology, the metres are personified and have their own narratives of origin.
2. *non-clinging*: The idea here is that the axe of non-attachment, like the knife of wisdom in 4.42, makes the form of the *ashvattha*, and therefore the spread of 'clinging action' on earth, barely perceptible.
3. *. . . to that imperishable place*: Verses 2–5 are in the *trishtubh* metre.
4. *the sixth [sense] is the mind*: See n. 4 to the Thirteenth Discourse.
5. *the lord*: Here again this is understood to be the self – *purusha* from the *samkhya* perspective and *atman* from the Upanishadic one.
6. *Soma*: See n. 5 to the Ninth Discourse. Various scholarly theories have opined that it was a mushroom, but its full identity remains unknown. In contemporary sacrificial revivals a milkweed plant stalk is used.

SIXTEENTH DISCOURSE

1. *'It is caused by desire!'*: There were many philosophical interlocutors during this time who understood there to be no sacred source to the world. Neither the Vedas, nor the practice of sacrifice, nor a single deity to whom one gave devotion could function as such a source. Rather, the world was fuelled by desire alone. These thinkers were called *nastika*s or 'naysayers', literally the 'There is not' school.
2. *carries the mind like a chariot*: 'The chariot of the mind' is a common term for a wish or desire.
3. *without Vedic rules*: *Avidhi*. Presumably, these are people whose sacrifice is motivated by desire and pride. Similar traits were invoked in 16.10. Even though, earlier in the *Gita*, Krishna does focus on the ways in which sacrifice can become its own obsessive object, here he also emphasizes the importance of knowing the rules if one is going to sacrifice to begin with. As Robert Minor (*Bhagavad Gītā: An Exegetical Commentary* (New Delhi: Heritage Books, 1982), 443) surmises, it may well be that those who sacrifice to gods other than Krishna are the problem here, as 9.23 also suggests. But regardless of the implications of this verse, the importance of knowing the general Vedic rules is emphasized in 16.23–4.
4. *This is the threefold . . . and desire*: It is fairly clear that at this period there was an emerging understanding of hell (*naraka*) as a space in which the transmigrating self moved because of its own clinging nature. However, it may well be a more metaphorical usage here, dealing with the permanent state of dissolution that is caused by anger, desire and greed. See also 1.42 and 16.16.

SEVENTEENTH DISCOURSE

1. *trust*: The word I have translated as 'trust' is *shraddha*. It is frequently translated as 'faith'. However, in much English usage, the term 'faith' implies an opposition to 'fact'. Moreover, 'faith' is often used in Jewish and Christian contexts to mean a creedal position. In contrast, the Sanskrit term *shraddha* implies a confidence in the workings of gods and human beings, a sense of trust in the nature of the universe and at times a sense of well-being.
2. *The sattvic people . . . rage and desire –*: Both verses 5 and 6 seem

to be making arguments against extreme forms of asceticism, as the Buddha also did. Such asceticism, as we saw in 3.6, is still caught up with clinging and desire for results.

3. *Om tat sat*: As mentioned in note 4 to the Seventh Discourse, 'Om' is the primordial sound and its three letters represent the threefold nature of the cosmos. *Om tat sat* means literally 'Om that real'. In essence, 'Om' is a truth which has all the qualities of *sattva*: pureness, light and clarity. One nominal sentence that is frequently used here is 'Om is that [which is] truth.'

THE EIGHTEENTH DISCOURSE

1. *Bristling-Haired One, Killer of Keshin*: There may be a word-play here in the use of two epithets for Krishna: *hrishikesha*, 'The Bristling-Haired One', and *keshinishudana*, 'Killer of Keshin', a demon who was slain by Vishnu in the *Mahabharata* (Krishna here is an *avatara* of Vishnu).
2. *contrary to custom*: As the *Gita* has reiterated many times, action that presumes to go against the grain of what is socially acceptable is still action, and can produce fruits.
3. *Listen properly to these, also*: Krishna is now winding up his discourse on the *guna*s and is referring more and more to the kind of action Arjuna *himself* should perform: enlightened action, tempered with wisdom.
4. *the three grades of joy*: Sattvic 'joy', or joy that comes from the highest *guna* of *sattva*, is not a changing, clinging, form of happiness. Rather, it is the deep joy of one who does not cling at all. This kind of joy was also described in 14.27.
5. *All beginnings . . . by smoke*: This teaching is prevalent in many different venues of early Indian thought, and is very different from Jewish, Christian and Muslim concepts of creation and order. In Indian texts, the first sacrifice, while auspicious, did not result in perfect order. The first creation by the god Prajapati was also in error and needed another attempt to be successful. Order is understood as emerging incrementally; creation is a realistic matter of trial and error and reaching procedural perfection over time.
6. *the objects of sense, starting with sound*: They begin with sound (*shabda*) and include a sense of touch (*sparsha*), a sense of visual form (*rupa*), a sense of taste (*rasa*) and a sense of smell (*gandha*).

Because of the primacy of sound in early Indian thought, one usually begins with hearing.

7. . . . *I will speak for your benefit*: As the *Gita* finishes, Krishna moves from a discussion of equanimity and yogic discipline to one of *bhakti*, or devotion to Krishna.

8. *Hari*: A common epithet of Krishna. It is also an epithet of Vishnu, and, as stated earlier, Krishna is an *avatara* of Vishnu. Thus the use of the epithet might imply the greatness of Vishnu in many forms.